IT Capstone Project

third edition

A Workbook for Senior Design Projects I & II

Peter J. Farrell

Information Sciences &
Technology Department
George Mason University

Kendall Hunt
publishing company

Kendall Hunt publishing company

www.kendallhunt.com
Send all inquiries to:
4050 Westmark Drive
Dubuque, IA 52004-1840

ISBN: 978-1-5249-0471-5

Published in the United States of America

About the Author

Peter J. Farrell, MBA, is a faculty member in the Information Sciences & Technology Department, Volgenau School of Engineering at George Mason University in Fairfax, Virginia. Mr. Farrell is the course coordinator for the Information Technology Capstone series of undergraduate junior- and senior-level courses. He is alum of George Mason University. He has an undergraduate degree in accounting and a master's degree in business administration, with a concentration in information systems.

Mr. Farrell was a Certified Public Accountant and spent most of his professional career managing large commercial and government information technology projects. He has had roles as Vice President of Finance, Vice President of Sales, and Senior Vice President of Information Technology at US-based firms before joining the faculty at Mason.

Table of Contents

Acknowledgments

I am most appreciative of my George Mason Capstone faculty for their willingness to share their experience and time with our students, and their ideas with me. I am particularly indebted to colleagues David Richard and Thomas Arnsperger for their review of this workbook and their advice.

Introduction

This workbook, *IT Capstone Project*, is designed to provide an overview of the Senior Design Capstone process. A careful reading of the text will provide the context and steps in defining, organizing, and developing a successful project.

Completing a Senior Design Capstone project will prepare the student for the environment found in many IT firms. Making the transition from the university to the rigors of the work environment is challenging for any student. This is no less true for the technically trained student. Technical students possess a unique set of skills and are often thrust into situations where senior managers are involved. The capstone experience is designed to prepare technical students to be effective in demonstrating their technical and communications skills.

The IT capstone experience is composed of three sequential one-semester courses:

Course 1: IT Project Management—A one-semester course on managing a successful IT project as a project manager.

Course 2: Senior Design I—This semester is focused on understanding a client's business and the issues facing the business. The approach to accomplish this objective is described in Part l of this workbook.

Course 3: Senior Design II—The final course is concerned with selecting, developing, and implementing a solution for the client's business. This process is described in Part ll of this workbook.

This series of courses is designed to afford an undergraduate information technology student with exposure to the steps for evaluating and improving a business process in an actual client's business setting. In this sequence of courses, the information technology component is secondary to understanding the business, understanding the competitive environment, analyzing business processes, and providing an approach for improving those processes.

At this stage of an engineering student's education, the skills involved in developing and implementing an information technology solution should be mature. The capstone courses strive to have student teams view the business as encompassing the broader perspective of an operating entity rather than the narrow focus of the information technology underpinnings of the business.

As a basis, the three courses are designed to help the students meet the following learning objectives:

Learning objectives for IT Project Management are as follows:

1. Understand the importance of project management in improving the success of information technology projects.
2. Understand the constraints of project management.
3. Learn tools and techniques of project management, including communications through written documentation.

Learning objectives for Senior Design Project I and Senior Design Project II are as follows:

1. Learn to plan for and manage the delivery of a successful meeting.
2. Analyze a business process and identify the business challenges.
3. Quantify the impact of a business challenge within a business process.
4. Identify unfulfilled opportunities and benefits caused by a process challenge.
5. Plan and deliver effective sales and situation briefings and presentations.
6. Develop an effective project team.
7. Understand the importance of leading peers to create an effective team.

In addition to the course content, the class is designed to help students develop capabilities that are critical to being business professionals, including teamwork, research, critical thinking, and oral and written communications skills.

The three courses, IT Project Management followed by Senior Design Project I and Senior Design Project II, build on one another. The sequence of these courses is critical to build a set of skills to develop and present a successful business case for change, that is, changing the business for the better. Figure 1.0 shows the suggested approach in building this skill set.

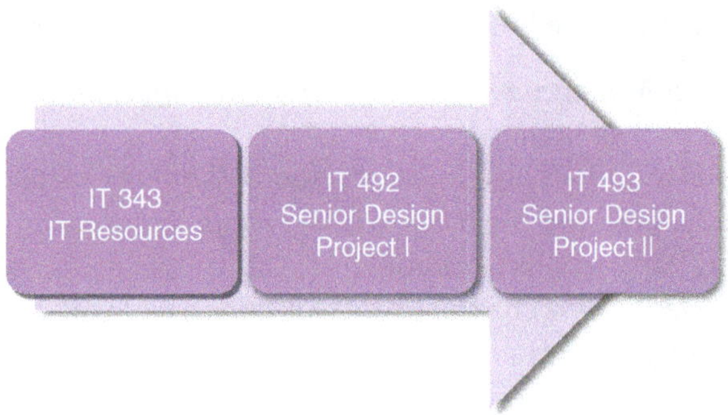

• **Figure 1–0** Sequence of IT Capstone Courses

STUDENT AND FACULTY RESPONSIBILITIES

The student team partners with a client to identify business process issues, create detail plans, and implement solutions. The capstone program is a synthesis of the student's engineering education and general education. This is accomplished as a team of student engineers in the role of a consultant to the client business.

What student teams do:

- Meet with the client.
- Understand the business.
- Focus on business issues.
- Quantify the business issues.
- Set the scope of the project.
- Evaluate alternatives.
- Fashion a compelling solution.
- Develop the solution.
- Present the solution.

What the faculty provides:

- A structured process
- Defined elements of the analysis and implemented solution
- Guidance to the student team throughout the course

The remainder of the textbook will discuss the approach the student team should use to work with their client and to develop a solution to improve that business.

PART I

Making the Business Case for Change

CHAPTER 1

Introduction of the Business Case for Change

Chapter 1 is an introduction to the elements of the business case for change. These elements include defined class assignments that help the student team understand the processes of a business and to engage the client in a discussion of the business.

The first semester of the capstone courses, Senior Design Project I, focuses on identifying areas in the sponsor's business that have the potential for a positive change. The student project team needs to follow a set of analytical processes to successfully develop a business case for change. In general terms these step include

- An understanding of the client's business, the general business environment, the competitive environment, and the trends that might impact the client's business
- An evaluation and quantification (measurement) of a portion of the client's process
- Identification of elements that could be improved by technology and process changes
- Identification of technology elements that result in a positive impact on the client's business

This process starts with an understanding and analysis of the client's business. The team needs to have a solid understanding of the client's business, both the specific company and the business environment in which the client's business operates.

Chapters in this workbook will provide (1) a description on how to select a project, (2) ideas on how to organize a team, (3) the elements in developing a compelling business case for change, and (4) a sample presentation for both the first and second semesters.

The final expectations for Senior Design Project I, developing the business case for change, culminate in these activities:

1. Demonstrate that the team understands the client's business.
2. Demonstrate that the team understands the business problem, or problems, and can describe them.
3. Show how the team has quantified, that is, measured, the negative impact of the business problem.
4. Provide a high-level overview of potential solutions.
5. Develop and present the business, problem, quantification, and alternatives in a formal presentation to a panel of outside business leaders and faculty.
6. Complete a peer evaluation of team members.

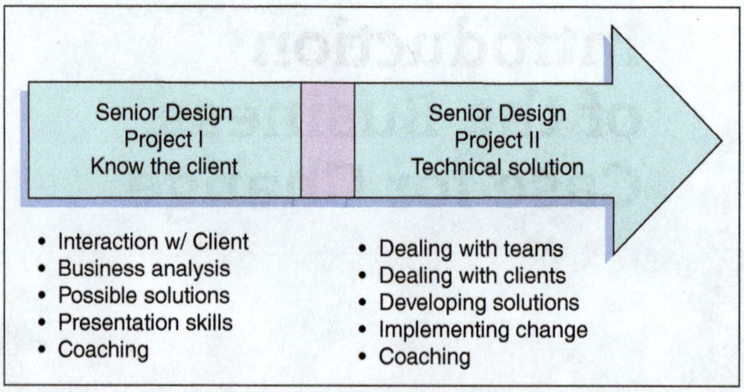

● **Figure 1–1** Overview of the Two Senior Design Project Semesters

The major component of the project is to understand the client's business, the business environment, and the area, or areas, of potential improvement. This broad perspective of the business and its processes can be a significant challenge for engineering students who only have a focus on applying information technology.

It is important to remember that the purpose of the project is to solve a business problem using information technology as a portion of the solution.

An overview of the capstone courses shows the progression of the two semesters (Figure 1–1).

The class activities to develop the business case for change are summarized in the scorecard used by the judging panel during the team's presentation at the end of the semester. The key elements are described below:

1. The enterprise is described: This covers areas like the nature of the business, the industry, services provided, ownership, complexity, legal or regulatory constraints on the business, if the business is profitable.
2. Business process described and quantified: This is a key method to understand the flow of the business and could include process flows, costs in personnel, time, material, and equipment. Quantification, as the term is used in this text, means the ability to measure the cost of the process. The analysis by the team in concert with the client should identify areas that can and should be improved. The most important and difficult element is quantifying the processes and ultimately quantifying the impact on improvements the team will propose. This is discussed in detail in a later chapter.
3. What can be improved by IT: Reviewing the work done in the first steps, the team should be in a position to identify and select areas for improvement.
4. Proposed solutions: This may be the easiest element for the team to define. There should be two or three well-researched options to present to the client.
5. Implementation challenges: Embracing change is difficult. The team's well-reasoned potential solutions will also face this resistance to change due to cultural, personnel, or implementation challenges. The team must address the challenges and develop mitigating steps to overcome the challenges.

The scorecard for the first semester of the capstone course, shown in Chapter 3, has the rating criteria for the final presentation and the associated weighting of each element. In most cases the semester-end presentation by the student team is a summary of several key elements the project team must develop during the semester. The final presentation for the semester is condensed to key ideas since the presentation is limited to 15 minutes. The restriction on allotted time is designed to help the team focus on and present only the key elements in their analysis of their client's business.

A critical element in a team's success in the course is the periodic observations and input from other teams in the class and from the faculty member. The scorecard used by the judging panel during the end of semester presentation is an excellent tool to use in evaluating and discussing the key elements of the team's project and progress.

As a supplement to the final presentation, each student team provides a notebook with additional details of meetings, client discussions, and research documents. The team notebook is typically organized in sections for (1) resumes of team members, (2) description of client, client business environment, documentation on business processes, (3) team meeting documentation, (4) client meeting documentation, (5) final presentation, and (6) research on technical solutions.

PROJECT SELECTION

Choosing a project is one of the most important decisions a team will make. The students work on the project for two semesters and the team will be working with the same client for both semesters. Selecting a project that has sufficient complexity and breadth is a factor in developing a robust analysis and solution and in being able to maintain the team's interest. We will discuss the formation of teams later in this chapter.

The most important consideration in selecting a project is that the project be centered on a business process, or strategy, that would benefit from improvement where part of the improvement is the introduction of technology. Projects can be categorized into two general types: (1) process improvement depicted in Figure 1–2 and (2) fundamental redesign in Figure 1–3.

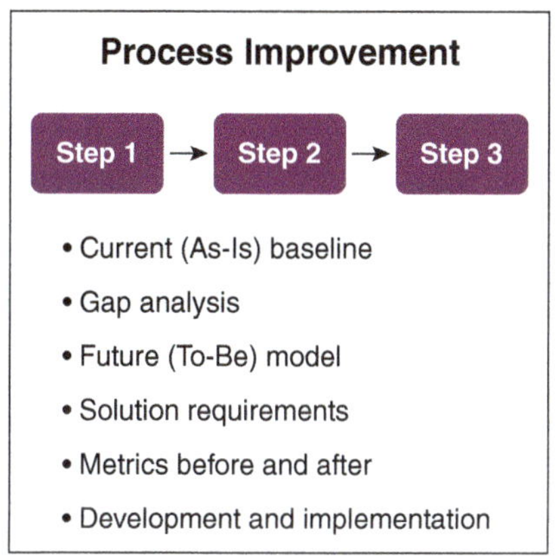

● **Figure 1–2** Process Improvement Project

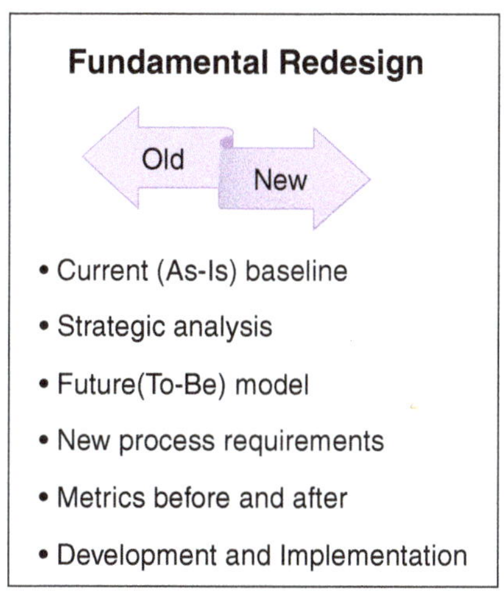

● **Figure 1–3** Fundamental Redesign Project

Projects come from two primary sources. Most projects come to the class in a vetting process within the student teams. Teams generate several project proposals and present those for evaluation with the instructor. These project ideas come from companies the students know or problem areas the students notice.

The second source of projects is from the capstone faculty. The faculty members have contacts to a variety of outside entities in their professional network. These outside projects can be presented to teams for their consideration. The teams, in concert with the instructor, will determine which projects are sufficiently complex that the business issues would result in a viable subject and provide for an interesting presentation at the conclusion of Senior Design Project l and Senior Design Project ll. Developing a web site is not a project of sufficient breadth to be considered as a potential project.

One common misconception is that having a student on the team with detailed knowledge of a potential client company is critical to the project being successful. There is little relationship between having that detailed exposure and a successful capstone project. The student team must understand the client business from a unique and detailed perspective. A student working in a firm may have some knowledge of how the client's operations work but he/she may not have an understanding of the business processes in the context of the business as a whole.

Most team members do not have detailed exposure to the prospective business in advance of the project. And yet teams are successful in identifying a likely process to improve, developing a business case for change, and defining viable solutions.

Projects that have been successfully executed in the past include

- Car rental return operations
- Inventory control systems for assets in a warehousing firm or in a retail operation
- Athletic organization coach's data and remote entry: including iPhone applications for training regiments, scheduling coaches, and membership tracking
- Nation-wide alumni web communications, reunion registration, and donor database solution
- Process improvement in numerous businesses including information security, online web shopping approaches, and various dashboards for critical data analysis.

PROJECT DIFFICULTY

Students should undertake projects that are both challenging and interesting. Challenging projects such as a difficult business environment or a complex set of business processes will provide the opportunity for the solution to be innovative and to have a substantial positive impact on the business. The difficulty of the project also provides a gauge to the potential final grade on the project.

A review of many completed projects provides a guide to the types of businesses that have generated projects that were easier and deserving of an average grade or more difficult and deserving of an above-average grade (Figure 1–4).

Projects that are easy typically lead to pedestrian solutions that are quite obvious early in the project, and the projects are likely to be limited in scope. As the project difficulty increases, solutions become more involved and the project has the potential for an innovative approach, leading to a more interesting solution and potentially a better grade.

Every project, every client, and every team is unique. An easy or intermediate project can be interesting and innovative as a result of the team's actions. For example, an easy project could develop into a much more interesting project with research that generates an innovative approach or solution, as indicated in Figure 1–5. In addition, a well-constructed

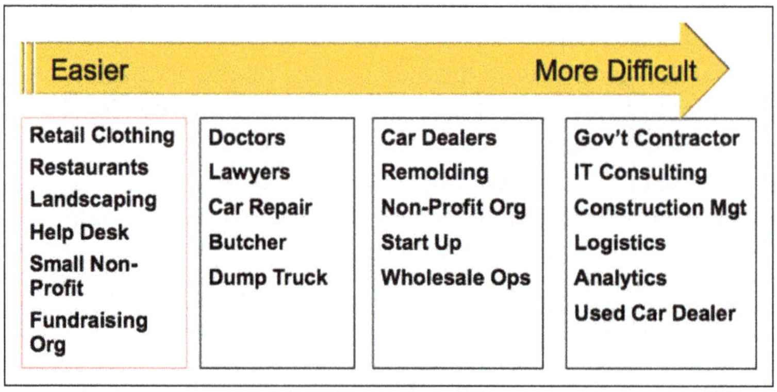

• **Figure 1–4** Scale of Project Difficulty

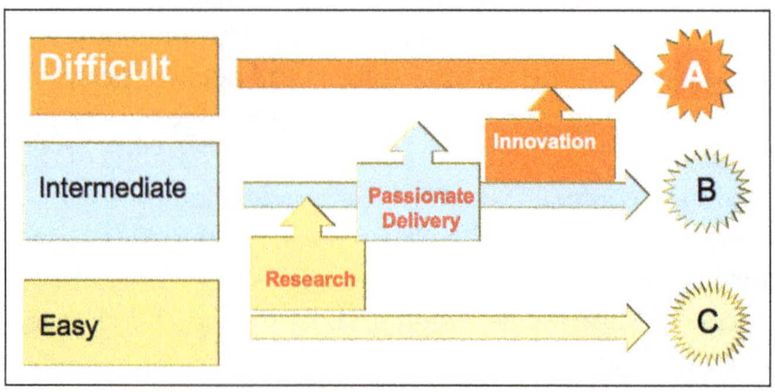

• **Figure 1–5** Project Difficulty Relative to Potential Grade presentation of the project, in both the first semester of the course and the second semester, can enhance the presentation judges' perception of the project leading to a higher evaluation of the project.

SELECTING THE TEAM PROJECT

It is challenging for a student team to select a project that has a willing client, some degree of difficulty, is interesting to research, and be the subject of an engaging presentation. The steps in selecting a team project are shown in Figure 1–6. Both the team and the faculty member contribute to the selection process, but ultimately the team must make the selection since it will be their focus for an entire year.

Each student is required to generate a project idea. The team and faculty will explore the facets of the potential projects to arrive at a preliminary understanding of the intent and scope of the projects. The capstone faculty member will have had significant experience with many previous projects, having served as a judge for several prior presentations. This selection process is a preliminary evaluation, based on a limited discussion with potential clients. It may be necessary to have an additional conversation with clients and conduct additional analysis by the team to arrive at a suitable team project.

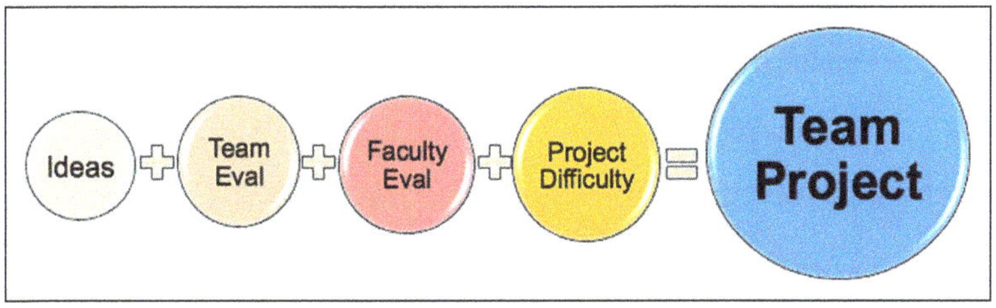

Figure 1–6 Steps in Selecting a Team Project

ASKING FOR A PROJECT

Generally, undergraduate information technology students arrive at the capstone courses with no experience in asking for a project, particularly in asking a client outside of the classroom environment. Most students find this particular task to be quite difficult. Part of the capstone course is experiencing this process of integrating their prior course work as a building block in their conversation with potential clients. In hindsight, many students report that this experience is beneficial in their preparation for the professional environment after graduation.

Even where students know a potential client or business, the students generally do not have the experience to approach potential clients in their search for a project. To prepare students for this task, they are provided with a corporate overview presentation to share with potential clients, a script for the discussion with potential clients, and a set of questions and answers potential clients might ask. The students also have a basic form to complete to capture information from an interested client.

The essence of the corporate overview includes these elements that will assist the students in establishing the basic tenants of the potential project:

- Senior Design projects are business process consulting engagements by information technology undergraduate seniors.
- There is a minimal investment of your time. Our faculty members are active advisors and mentors to the team.
- The analysis and results are completely free. The client has no obligation to implement the solution but many do.
- Business process reengineering projects are analyzed, researched, packaged, tested, and presented.

- It is a two-semester (9-month) project.
- Senior teams of five, six, or seven information technology engineers trained in networks, databases, web development, and cyber security will work on the project.

If a client is interested in participating as a potential team project, the student will complete the project information form, providing as much information as is garnered in this initial contact with the client. The student, in consultation with the client, may not be able to address all the questions on the form.

Capstone Project Proposal

Project Name: ____________________

Sponsoring Organization: ____________________

Organization Point of Contact: ____________________

Phone: ____________________ Email: ____________________

1. What is the challenge?
2. What is its effect on the organization and/or customers?
3. What does a perfect solution look like?
4. What are the critical parameters of change (time, funding, people)?

Once the student team is formed one of their first tasks is to vet potential projects. A few key questions will help the student team evaluate which projects will be adequately challenging and will lead to a successful engagement. The important questions are as follows:

1. Is the client committed to a project with the student team?
2. Are there business issues?
3. Does the business issue involve data security, process organization, web design, and database structure and technology infrastructure?
4. Can the student team fashion an interesting presentation from the business, the issue, and the solution?
5. Can the project scope be completed in two semesters?
6. Does the client have the time to invest with the student team?

Students should spend a significant amount of effort in both selecting a project and preparing the client for the process. Client management is discussed in the next section.

CLIENT MANAGEMENT

During the project selection process, the student or several students make initial contact with the client. These first impressions are important. The ability to manage a client's expectation during the project will have a significant impact on the success of the team's efforts and the level of engagement with the client. Client management begins with setting expectations for the client and establishing a schedule for client meetings.

The course assignments that follow lend structure to the course. The student team can use this list of activates to establish a structure for the project from the viewpoint of the client. The requirement to interact with the client and gather specific information is one of the important learning objectives of the Senior Design Project. The objective is to learn to ask focused questions and conduct professional interviews. The assignments are designed to require input from the client to complete, in particular assignments 2, 3, 5, and 6.

Assignment 1. Introduction by team lead:
- Prepare an introduction of the team.
- Present the project in one or two slides.
- Summarize your project plan for the semester in one slide.

Assignment 2. Business and competition:
- Description of the client's business.
- Local and national competition and trends.

Assignment 3. Processes described and quantified:
- Description of the client's processes (flow chart or similar comprehensive view of the business).
- Metric and evaluation method for "As Is" and "To Be."
- Comparison of "As-Is" measurement to the forecast of "To Be," that is, improved process. This is the compelling case for change.

Assignment 4. What can be improved by IT:
- Entire As-Is process considered.
- Solution requirements (cost, time, people, training).
- Identify the technical skills used in the various options proposed.

Assignment 5. Proposed solutions:
- Description of *three* options to address or improve the client's process.
- Describe the "To-Be" process.
- Describe any innovative approaches or techniques involved in solution.

Assignment 6. Implementation challenges:
- Business cultural challenges
- Financial, time, people, training, and sustainment.
- Client acceptance criteria for the solution.
- IT 493 development and implementation schedule.
- Risks and mitigation plans.

Once the project has been selected, the first project-oriented client contact should occur. An initial timeframe for client interaction could be set using the assignments from the Senior Design Project l class. This will parallel the class syllabus and insure that client interaction will correspond to team deliverables.

Many teams will develop a more formal arrangement with the client that could include a written charter with specific milestones and deliverables identified. Client interface dates and deliverables will be included in the team's schedule. The most significant and challenging deliverables are discussed in the next chapter. The team needs a significant amount of information from the client in order to build an effective business case for change. The business case for change shows the client the potential positive impact of the change proposed by the team.

The information gathered in this research may be of a proprietary nature, that is, the client would not want the data to be shared with a competitor. The team should ensure that client information is properly protected during the project.

There are areas where a client might direct, or even insists, on a particular direction or solution. This direction may detract from the team's efforts and consume time to investigate. The student team should have the viewpoint of outside and independent consultants bring their unique technical skills and business understanding to a project. In many situations the client has a clear bias toward a certain approach or even a certain solution. The team should maintain an independent perspective in looking for their best approach, and ultimately their recommended solution.

FORMING THE TEAM

Developing a successful Senior Design Project requires a business situation that is interesting and challenging, a team of students with a mix of technical and social skills, along with the team infrastructure, to blend the project research and analysis into an effective solution. Most projects will encompass elements of software development, web development, database development, data security and networking, in addition to mapping business processes. A team with expertise in these areas or access to these skills is critical. The team selection is led by the instructor to ensure a reasonable mix of technical and personal skills. Members of the team select their team's lead.

Students with the necessary technical skills are typically available for the team, although care must be exercised in selecting members with the breadth of skills required for the project. In addition to technical skills, personalities are important to the ability of a team to have adequate exchange of ideas. There are many personality evaluation methods available that could be used in selecting team members.

As a guide, a solid student team with the requisite technical skills can be constructed using the table in Figure 1–7.

Once the team members are identified, the team should select a team lead. The team lead position varies by team from merely a coordinator, to a position that directs the detailed assignments and processes of the team. Being a team lead is demanding even on a well-organized and motivated team. In circumstances where the team lacks focus or motivation, being a team lead can be quite demanding and time consuming.

The team needs to get organized and get started on their project. Effective time management is an important factor in successful student teams. The following are the necessary steps to plan and start working on the project:

Plan: The key element in planning is to establish the scope of the project based on the class schedule, project proposal, and feedback from the instructor. A high-level schedule can be fashioned from the class assignments shown earlier in this chapter and the project milestones from the course syllabus. Most major presentations will be clearly identified in the class syllabus.

Initialize: Tasks and Task Owners—An early deliverable from the team is a schedule for the semester. This should be a GANTT chart with sufficient detail to identify the significant tasks for the semester such as documents to be completed, client meetings, team meetings, milestones, deliverables to the client, and presentations. This initial project plan could be viewed as a project encompassing just the first semester or as

	Security	Web	DB	Network	Business minor
Member 1	✓				
Member 2		✓			
Member 3			✓		
Member 4				✓	✓
Member 5	✓				
Member 6				✓	

• **Figure 1–7** Team Member Skill Selection Chart

a composite for both semesters. A reasonable approach is to focus on only the first semester since significant changes will occur as the first semester unfolds.

A particular challenge in a recently formed team is to determine the strengths of the team members, including who should be the team lead. The process within each team to identify the best use for team members needs to be resolved in the first or second team meeting because the team must begin making progress to remain within the time constraints of the semester.

Establishing the schedule early in the semester will allow the team to develop a realistic gauge of the time constraints they face in understanding the business, quantifying the current processes, and looking for potential areas for improvement, in addition to preparing the various status and final presentation material. A team schedule may look similar to the following sample schedule. Key elements that should be added include the time estimate for each task, the task dependencies, and the team member or members assigned to each task.

Senior Design Project I Sample Schedule		
1.0	**Project Selected**	
2.0	**Develop Work Plan**	
	2.1	Develop Work Breakdown Structure
	2.2	Develop Project Staffing Plan
	2.3	Develop Project Schedule
	2.4	Develop Project Budget
3.0	**Initial Meeting with Client**	
	3.1	Prepare Agenda and Client Questions
	3.2	Discuss Project Timeline with Client
	3.3	Gather initial Client Data
	3.4	Set next Meeting Date and Agenda
	3.5	Document Client Meeting
4.0	**Document As-Is State of Business**	
	4.1	Develop Survey Method
	4.2	Walk though High-Level Business Processes
	4.3	Document In Detail the Targeted Process
	4.4	Establish Quantification Measurements
	5.4	Document Review and Follow-up Questions
5.0	**Evaluate Business Environment**	
	5.1	Research Business Competition
	5.2	Develop Ranking method
	5.3	Team Meeting to rank and select solution
	5.4	Document Team Meeting

Continued

Senior Design Project I Sample Schedule		
6.0	Team Status Presentation	
7.0	Identify Potential Business Process for Improvement	
8.0	Quantify Business Process	
9.0	Develop Business Case for Change	
10.0	Team Status Presentation	
11.0	Develop High-Level Solution Alternatives	
12.0	Team Status Presentation	
13.0	Prepare and Present Draft Presentation	
14.0	Complete Team Notebook	
15.0	Prepare and Present Final Presentation	

A best practice is to assign each task to an individual team member so accountability is established. The same approach should be followed at the major topic level, not just for the individual tasks. As an example, the overall quantification of the business process can be the major task of a particular team member. The team member may evaluate the client's business process and assign another team member to research the competitive landscape of the business.

A critical decision made by the team is the scope of their project. The faculty will assist in defining the scope to be sufficiently encompassing that the project is challenging, but is also a project that can be completed within the capstone course.

Looking ahead to the second semester, Senior Design Project ll, developing and implementing the project will take a substantial amount of time and energy. Therefore, setting the initial parameters of the project is an important team effort. The scope may increase or decrease as the team becomes more familiar with the client and the processes within the client company.

Communications across the team is critical. A typical team of five or six students will meet in person or electronically once or twice a week in addition to client meetings and class meetings. The team lead is usually the organizer and a significant amount of the lead's time is involved in coordination efforts. Teams need to establish their meeting and contact protocol at their first meeting. At a minimum, the team needs to set up a mechanism for setting up meetings, posting items to review, gathering research documents, group presentations, client meetings, and schedule updates.

Quickly establishing the team infrastructure, client interaction, and a viable schedule is a key objective once the project has been selected. A prior semester's Senior Design Team is often invited back as guest lecturer. The constant theme from the prior teams in their lessons learned is the importance of time management. A team must quickly become adept at understanding, consolidating, and presenting the project status within a very short time horizon.

WHEN TO ASK FOR HELP

Teams, and particularly team leads, are new to their team and to the demands of a time-sensitive project. An important lesson to be learned is when to ask for help from the faculty member. The experience of working with clients as a consultant is challenging, as is working with team members who have varying skills and demands on their time. The Senior Design Project has two safeguards to bring the need for assistance to the fore. The first safeguard is the requirement for frequent periodic status reporting to the class and the faculty. The second safeguard is the peer review process.

The Senior Design Project is about preparing students for their professional environment. Evaluating progress toward that preparation is an important objective. This peer evaluation involves not only the faculty but the student team members as well. At the end of each of the two semesters of the Senior Design Project, students are required to submit an evaluation of each of their team members. This submission is not shared with the students but serves to focus faculty attention on both positive and negative situations within a team.

LOOKING AHEAD

Throughout Chapter 1 the activities focus on setting up the project and the infrastructure. The discussion on client management emphasizes the importance of setting expectations. Student deliverables are no less important. These are the documents that the teams will produce as evidence of the successful first semester project. These elements will be explained further in Chapter 2, "Establishing the As-Is State," and Chapter 3, "Making the Case for Change."

QUESTIONS AND CASE STUDY FOR CHAPTER 1

1. What are three of the learning objectives for the capstone courses?
2. What factors should be considered in selecting a Senior Design Project?
3. What is a peer review and how is it used in the capstone courses?
4. What are the sources for a team developing a Senior Design Project I schedule?

Case Study: A team has two potential projects to evaluate. Project A is a small business that has had modest growth over the last few years but is in a technology field that has experienced significant growth over a similar period. Project B is a multi-location storefront retail business. The firm in Project B has no online footprint but in-store sales remain steady.

1. What factors and issues might the team consider in choosing between these two projects? You may make assumptions but disclose the assumptions and their impact on the selection process.
2. How could the team improve their knowledge of the businesses in order to improve their selection?
3. Which project is likely to be a process improvement project and which is likely to be a fundamental redesign project?

CHAPTER

2 The As-Is Situation and the Problem

Chapter 2 discusses how to evaluate the client business that was selected for the capstone project. This evaluation includes the steps of establishing the "As-Is" or current state of the business. The As-Is state of the business will be important in determining the areas to improve.

In Chapter 1 the project was selected and the team infrastructure established. Now we examine the central theme of the first semester, analyzing, identifying, and quantifying, that is, measuring, business processes. The important question is which processes should be improved? And how do you quantify that improvement, meaning how can the positive impact be measured in monetary terms? This positive impact is the business case for change. Few business owners would want to change just for the sake of change, so the business case for change illustrates to the client the potential positive impact of the changes proposed by the team.

The majority of the learning objectives shown in Chapter 1 are imbedded in the challenge of determining and quantifying the business case for change. Information gathered and decisions made in this phase will carry into the project in the second semester. Therefore, a thorough understanding of the approach in this chapter is important.

As a reminder, the learning objectives in Senior Design Project I and in Senior Design Project II are a set of sequential processes of applying technical skills and project management skills developed during the undergraduate technical engineering experience.

In this chapter the current business situation, called the As-Is state of the business, is established. This will lead to the determination of the problem area, or areas, to be addressed by the team and the approach to quantifying the problem. Quantification will be a key point of comparison from the As-Is state to the improved To-Be state of the business process affected by the revised approach developed during the second semester of the Senior Design Project.

The capstone series of courses is akin to being the project manager of a technology project. The team completes a feasibility study and establishes the high-level requirements in Senior Design Project I. The team develops and implements the solution in Senior Design Project II. The steps are similar to that of any project subject to the constraints associated with a technology project. These constraints are (1) setting the scope of the project and (2) understanding the time available to complete the project. Time management is typically the most difficult challenge. The steps for the team to develop the project can be summarized as in Figure 2–1.

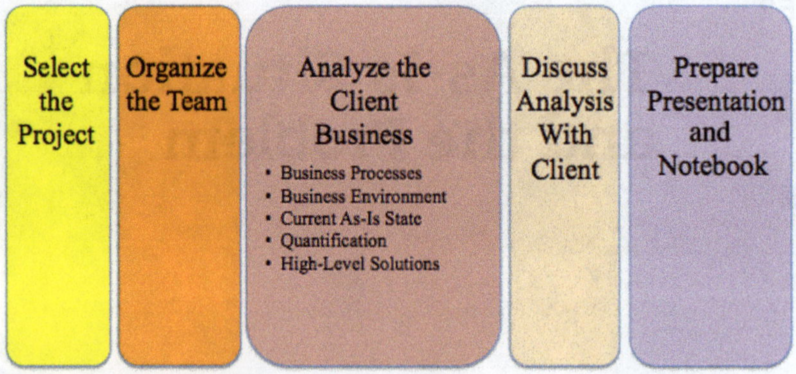

• **Figure 2–1** Senior Design Project Steps

Each business and each project is unique so only a general approach to understanding the business process can be described in this workbook. In spite of the uniqueness of the business situation, the team should consider the following general steps for a successful Senior Design Project l:

1. *Select the Project*—Each student is required to generate an idea and to initiate contact with the potential client. Based on information gathered on the New Project Form, the student team should have an idea of the business processes that are candidates for evaluation. Student teams will vet the various project ideas based on difficulty, interest, potential issues, and client interaction. In addition, the faculty will vet the best ideas to help the team make a final project selection.
2. *Organize the Team*—This should be a priority and was discussed in Chapter 1. Organization includes developing a baseline schedule and identifying task ownership.
3. *Analyze the Business*—The team should arrange for a client meeting for the purpose of gathering sufficient client intelligence to be able to document the business process, or processes, under investigation. The team needs to gather details on the processes that will provide the team with the quantitative information such as time involved, manpower used, paperwork prepared, and cost.
4. *Discuss Analysis with Client*—This step will allow the client to validate the analysis based on his/her knowledge of the business and the business environment.
5. *Prepare Notebook and Presentations*—The final activity is to document the semester's work in the team notebook and in the final presentation. These are covered in later chapters.

ESTABLISHING THE AS-IS SITUATION

MAJOR STEPS IN UNDERSTANDING A CLIENT'S BUSINESS

The team must establish an understanding of the business, the business environment, and the business processes as the initial step in developing ideas on what changes could benefit the client's business.

The steps involved in understanding the business generally include the analysis of the business as described in the following steps:

a. *Client Business Processes*—Client processes can be documented using various tools and will be the underpinnings of the current business processes depicted in the draft and final presentations as identified in the Senior Project Design l presentation shown in Chapter 4.
b. *Client Business Environment*—The team needs to understand the client's business, but also needs to understand the environment in which the business operates. This

is an important constraint to potential solutions. For example, if the industry direction is toward teleworking to save costs on facilities, then a potential solution should include the ability to work remotely so the client can remain cost competitive.

c. *Documentation of Business Processes*—The team will have to document the processes used by the business. An understanding of the processes is important to identify issues in the current process and to assist the team in developing an effective solution. Various tools are available to accomplish this documentation. These tools include detailed meeting notes, process diagrams, and client documentation.

   A benefit of having thorough documentation is to validate that the solution implemented during the second semester resolves the problems identified by the team.

d. *Current (As-Is) State*—At this point, the team should have a solid perspective of the client's business processes and the problem area or areas. The team is now ready to select the area they will address in their project. The team will need to quantify the problem and focus on potential solutions. Selection of solutions is discussed in Chapter 3.

e. *Quantification*–Quantification, as the term is used in this text, means the *ability to measure the cost of the process. Cost is the monetary impact* to the business to complete the process.

   In addition to the general steps briefly described here, later in this chapter we will discuss methods for quantification of the problem and for using the As-Is quantification as validation of the impact of the solution after the implementation of the solution.

f. *Potential High-Level Solutions*—Based on (1) the issues identified, (2) the client, (3) the business environment, and (4) the constraints documented by the team, the team should establish several potential solutions at a high level. This is discussed in Chapter 3. These potential solutions will be evaluated in detail during the following semester.

g. *Discuss Analysis with Client*—The team will conduct several meetings with the client. This step is included to emphasize that the team should review the business case for change with the client and review the requirements for the high-level solution. The detailed solution is a topic for Senior Design Project II.

h. *Presentation*—One objective of the previous steps is to build the elements that will become the basis of the formal presentation and the team notebook.

These steps closely correspond to the Senior Project Design l scorecard. Similar steps exist for the process for Senior Design Project ll as will be described in a later chapter. One objective of these steps is to compile organized documentation. The documentation will be used both in the team's notebook and as a basis for the following semester's requirements.

Later in this chapter there is a discussion on understanding the business and associated processes, which must be quantified, that is, measured, in monetary terms. The result of this careful analysis will lead to the identification of potential areas for improvement. Chapter 3 focuses on developing potential high-level solutions to improve these areas in the To-Be (future) state of the business.

Both the analysis of the business (Chapter 2) and the development of possible solutions (Chapter 3) are closely related, and both are required to forecast the To-Be (future) state of the business. The segregation of Chapters 2 and 3 into separate chapters is merely to allow students to focus on one of these two key elements at a time.

Do not consider potential high-level solutions before completing a thorough analysis of the business.

An effective review of a business can follow many approaches. One approach is described in the following section that will help the team understand and document the current state of the business. This analysis is used to determine which business processes are candidates for improvement in process flow, process execution, or application of technology. The team needs to quantify the target processes in its current state, the As-Is state, to set a benchmark from which to measure their improvements implemented in the second semester.

As a prelude to this discussion, ensure that costs, not just hours, are included in the analysis. Many business processes are easily measured using the time it takes to complete a task. This measurement of time will frequently be the initial approach to analyzing a process. However, time saved often does not translate to costs saved for the business. Saving time will only improve a business if the time saved is invested in improving the business such as increased marketing or new product development.

The first step in establishing the current state of the business, also called the "As-Is" state, is to understand the external business environment, the competitive environment, as well as the processes that exist within the business. As an example, a simple business is shown in Figure 2–2. The figure shows the business environment and establishes the areas to be analyzed for improvements and for quantification as described in the next section. These areas or processes must be measured in numeric terms and in a manner that can be re-measured after the project solution is implemented in the next semester. This re-measurement will establish the fact that the solution improved the process.

Step One: Understanding the Overall Business: The team needs to understand both the business and the business environment, for example, the competitive landscape, in order to evaluate the business processes within the company but also to understand the pressures from the competition or from trends impacting the client business. This is typically accomplished by discussion with the client and by researching similar businesses locally and nationally. The resulting documentation of this review can be a flow diagram, a very simple example of which is shown in Figure 2–2.

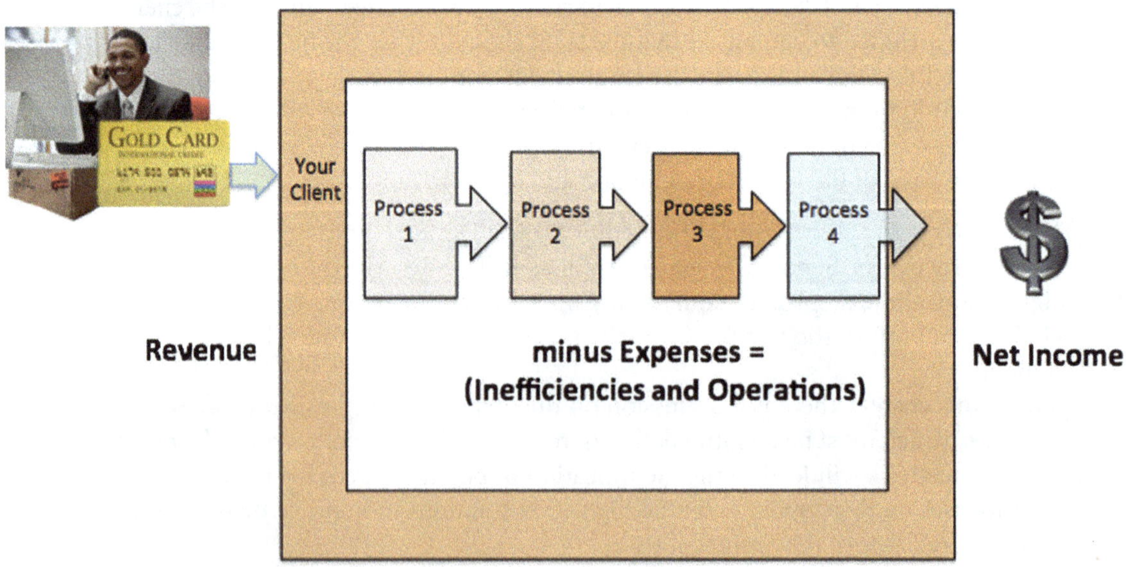

Photo © EdBockStock/Shutterstock.com

• Figure 2–2 Step One: Understanding the Context of the Business Processes

Step Two: Identifying Areas for Improvement: Based on the review in step 1 and the research by the team, the team should identify areas for potential improvements. Analyzing the impact of these improvements is the focus on quantifying the business case for change. The client business must anticipate an improved state or there is no reason to replace Process 2 and 3 in the current business with a potential new process (Figure 2–3).

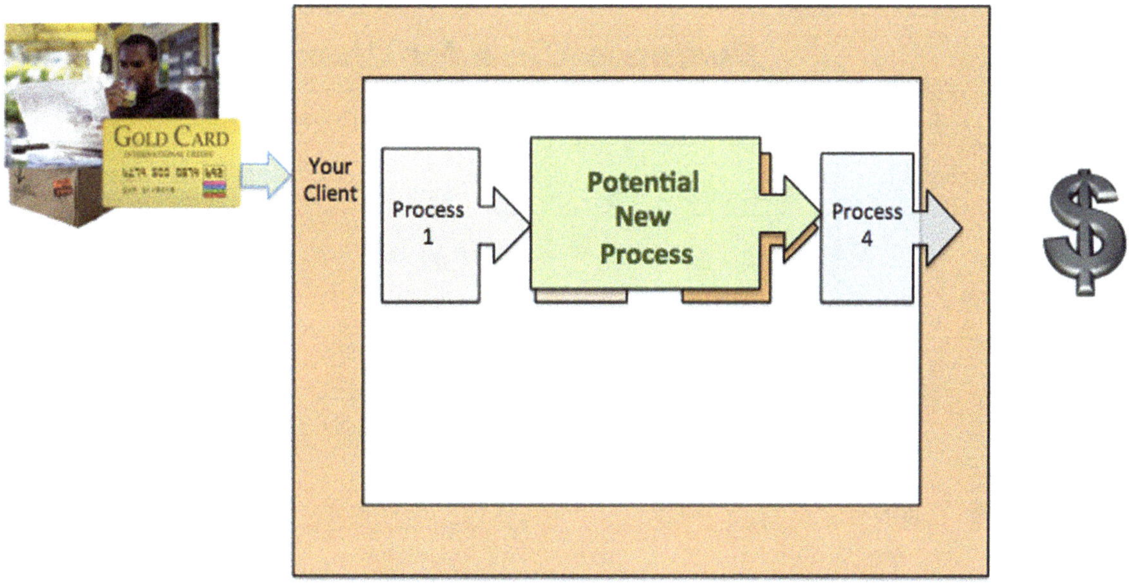

Photo © EdBockStock/Shutterstock.com

• **Figure 2–3** Step Two: Identifying Areas for Improvement

Step Three: Establishing the As-Is Situation with the proposed To-Be Situation: The final step in this example is a comparison of the current As-Is state of the business to the To-Be state anticipated after the improvements are implemented. The team will develop a method to quantify the current state, discussed in detail in the following section, as well as develop a forecast of the future "To-Be" state of the business. This comparison is shown graphically in Figure 2–4 and also in the form shown in Figure 2–5.

These simple examples show the process for analyzing a business. The actual process is significantly more difficult and time consuming. Gathering the necessary facts and figures will consume a substantial amount of the team's time during the semester.

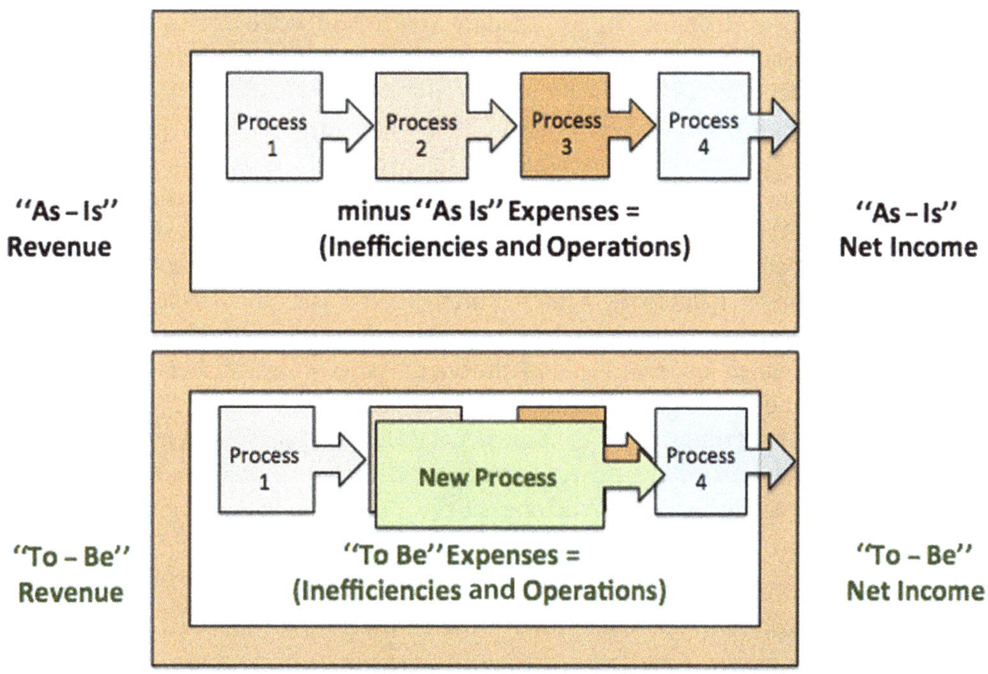

Photo © EdBockStock/Shutterstock.com

• **Figure 2–4** Step Three: Comparing the As-Is State to the To-Be State

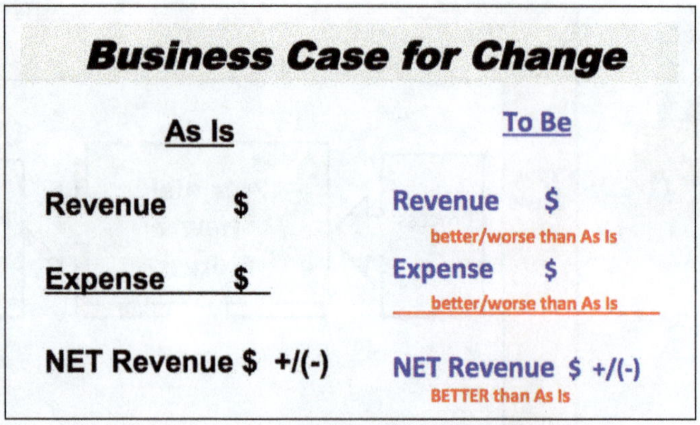

• **Figure 2–5** Business Case for Change Comparison

QUANTIFYING THE PROBLEM OR PROBLEMS

The most challenging aspect of the As-Is state is the ability to quantify the current state of the process. As was stated earlier, quantification means the *ability to measure the cost of the process. Cost is the monetary impact* to the business to complete the process. Measurement may also be in other numeric terms such as the error rate or the number of completed actions. But the goal is to establish the cost of those process, or errors, or tasks completed in terms of cost to the business.

Quantification is challenging because the approach to accomplish this is not always obvious, nor straightforward. Teams are not accustomed to the realm of numeric evaluations. A further complication is that the real-world nature of these projects introduces the notion of proprietary information: data that the client feels is sensitive from a competitive perspective. The client may be reluctant to disclose this type of information to the team or have the information disclosed to the class.

We will come back to this notion of data that is not available to the team but first let us look at various approaches to quantify the business problem. On a typical team, specific tasks are included in the schedule to quantify the As-Is and later the To-Be states and team members are assigned to this element of the overall solution and presentation.

A chart, Figure 2–5: Business Case for Change Comparison, is the essence of quantification. It compares the As-Is state (revenue less expenses equals net revenue) for the portion of the business process under evaluation to the future state, the To-Be state, which will exist after the team's solution is implemented. This data may be at the company level, at a department level, or at the isolated process level, depending largely on the focus of the project, the data available, the data collected in the interview process, and the analysis by the team of the client's business.

This simple chart (Figure 2-5) indicates that the numeric data of the As-Is state will, in the second semester, be compared to the To-Be state of the revised business process. A comparison of the state before improvement to the state after improvement is required to validate that the solution was an improvement and not a determent. Therefore, the method of gathering the data must be documented and repeatable by the team. As previously discussed, the To-Be forecast is dependent on the high-level solutions to be discussed in Chapter 3.

There are a variety of sources for quantitative data. Here is a list of just a few of the areas that could be useful in quantifying the As-Is state, but note that the items at the beginning of the list are easily quantifiable and the ones at the end of the list are more difficult to measure objectively:

- Lost revenue
- Missed customers
- Lost customers
- Time-consuming processes

- Sales too low
- Cost too high
- Too many staff
- Processes that cause lost time
- Theft of assets
- Misplaced inventory
- Buying the wrong items
- Customer satisfaction
- Employee morale

The team should be able to come to a resolution, after client interviews and the team's analysis, that the numeric evidence supports their contention that the problem area is the cause and the negative effect of the problem area has been identified. The team should be able to say, for example, one of the following statements.

Our client has (check one or more that apply)

❑ Low Revenue because of ____________________

❑ Losing Money because of ____________________

❑ Low Profits because of ____________________

❑ High Costs because of ____________________

❑ Losing customers because of ____________________

Figure 2-6 is a simple but explicit summary of a team's identification of the business problems uncovered. This element will be shown in the context of a complete presentation in Chapter 4, but is included here in Figure 2-6, because the team is addressing the key question in quantification—Why are we losing money?

This cause and effect is identified in Figure 2-7, and the monetary impact is shown in Figure 2-8. This is the business case for changing the problem area. The more significant

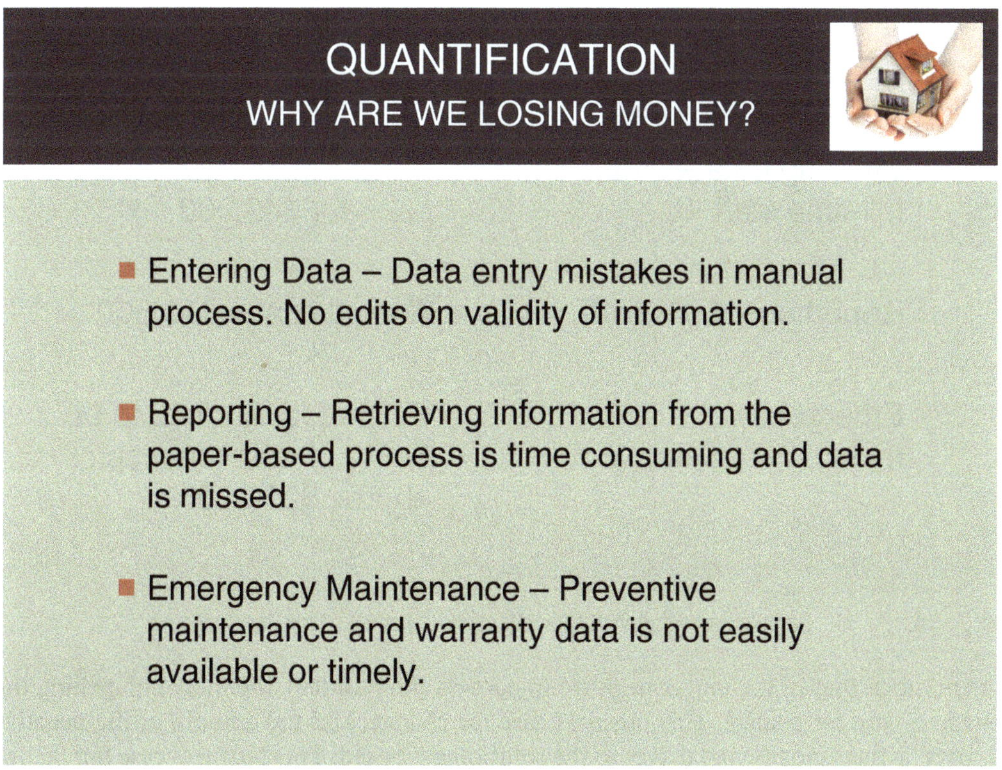

● **Figure 2-6** Presentation Example of Quantifying the Business Case

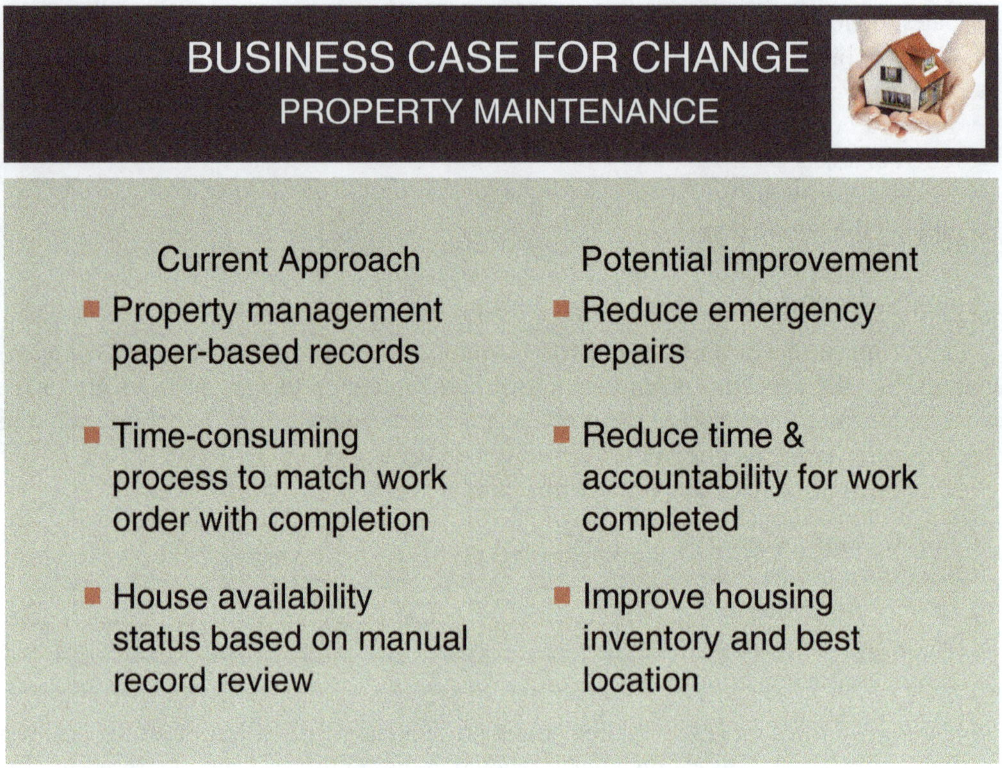

• **Figure 2–7** Sample Presentation Narrative of Business Case for Change

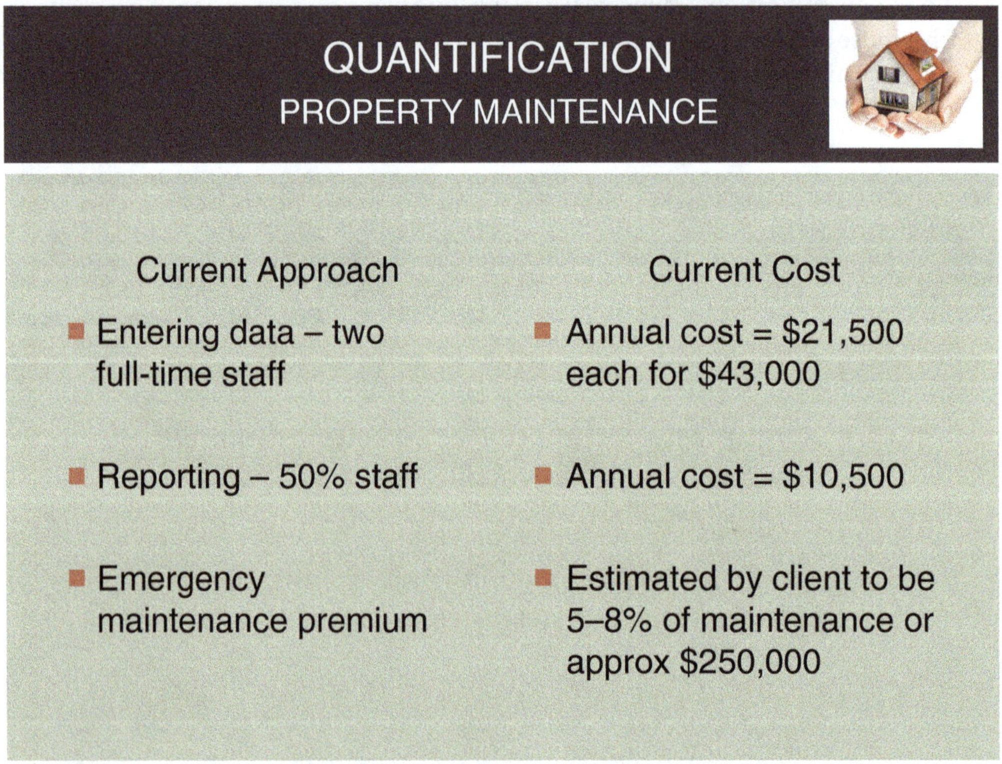

• **Figure 2–8** Sample Presentation of Quantification of Business Case for Change

the number, that is, the bigger negative impact on the business, the more compelling the business case for change. This business case for change, and the amount of the negative impact, is the fundamental driver to the solution proposed. This business case for change is shown in the context of the complete presentation again in Chapter 4 as Figure 4–7.

AMOUNT OF EVIDENCE NECESSARY FOR QUANTIFICATION

Not all business situations provide easily quantifiable cause and effect data. There are three broad categories of data the team could use for analysis of the client's business process. These categories are (1) directly measurable tangible data, (2) measurable but less tangible data, and (3) intangible data. Tangible data is generally the easiest to acquire, easiest to analyze, and easiest to compare. Examples of these data categories are as follows:

1. Directly Measurable = Tangible
   - **a.** Revenue/sales
   - **b.** Hours worked
   - **c.** Dollars collected
   - **d.** Cost of operations

     Examples of directly measurable factors:

     Workflow timesaving:
     - Savings in data entry = $21,000 (reduction of one position based on annual salary)
     - Reporting time saved = 4 hours per day or $10,500 per year (based on $21,000 per year salary)

     Device consolidation and floor space savings:
     - Reduced cost of maintenance agreements
     - Reduced cost of electricity
     - Lower cost per square foot of hospital space for dedicated printers and supply cabinets
2. Measurable but less Tangible
   - **a.** Workflow improvements
   - **b.** Redirected hours to more beneficial business processes
3. Indirectly Measured = Intangible
   - **a.** Customer satisfaction
   - **b.** Impact of new web page
   - **c.** Employee productivity
   - **d.** Reduced risk of fraud
   - **e.** Improved network security

     Examples of intangible cost factor calculations:

     Improved housing availability:
     - Better availability and better maintained housing units

     Increased IT manager's focus on more important issues and projects:
     - Device consolidation
     - Scalable solution
     - Consolidate to one source for equipment, service, and supplies

     Reduced exposure to internal prescription fraud and diversion:
     - Positioned for transition to direct links with vendors

The business case for change depends on the quantification of the As-Is state compared to the future To-Be state. If the business case for change cannot be based on tangible data, that is directly measurable, the analysis will potentially require multiple sources of data. If, for example, the quantification was of a new web page solution from the "Indirectly Measured = Intangible" category above, a team would have to develop some way to measure the impact of a web page before and after their solution is implemented.

It is necessary for the team to gather sufficient supporting evidence, typically research, to validate their contention that the team's proposed changes will have the desired positive impact on the client's business. As shown in the previous discussion, the more tangible and

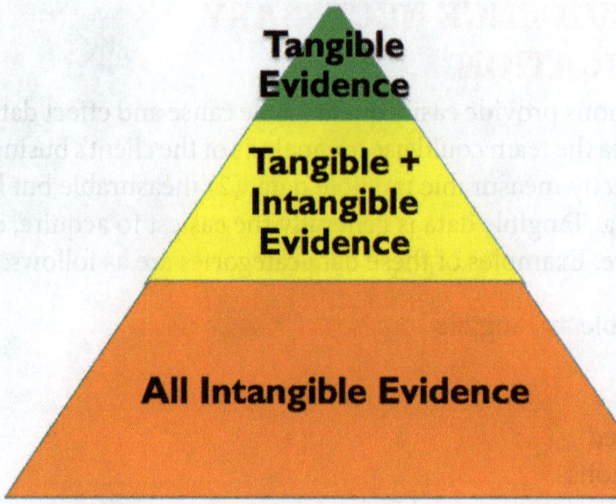

• **Figure 2–9** Amount of Supporting Evidence Triangle

easily measurable is the process, the less supporting evidence is needed. If the compelling business case for change is based on less directly measurable evidence the team needs to support their case with more data.

This level of supporting research can be shown graphically, as in Figure 2–9, which indicates the relative volume of support starting at the top of the triangle with the least area and therefore the smallest amount of evidence required. This indicates that the business case for change is based entirely on directly measureable tangible evidence. Conversely, if the business case were based primarily on intangible measurements, much more research and data would be needed to make a supportable argument.

In the instance of a business case dependent on intangible evidence, the team could use additional sources such as studies of similar web page implementations and the positive impact on business as a reasonable gauge of how their improvement would be expected to perform. However, since this approach is not directly measurable, a reasonable expectation is that the team will compile several relevant and closely related research documents to buttress their case for change.

An analysis only based on intangible data, such as employee morale, could be quantified by a survey. However, developing a survey might require skills in survey development and analysis that may not be available to the team. Reliance on a survey augmented by research might provide sufficient data to support the team's hypothesis of improvements.

The team, not the client, is responsible for gathering and analyzing the data that supports their business case for change. The validity of the information is also the responsibility of the team, not the client's. As part of the analysis, a prudent step would be to validate the information with the client for reasonableness. Estimates from the client or estimates of the positive impact of the team's implementation may turn out, upon further research, to be well outside the parameters of all similar firms and call into question the basis of the business case for change.

The last component in the quantification step is to consider how best to show this important set of numbers. The chart "Business Case for Change Comparison" shown in Figure 2–10 would be appropriate for easily quantifiable comparisons, but not all business cases for change are that straightforward. The team has only a brief amount of time to demonstrate all the elements in the scorecard at final presentation.

To support the quantification research, the team should use their notebook to document their data gathering and analysis methods. This will be useful in the second semester to develop comparative data.

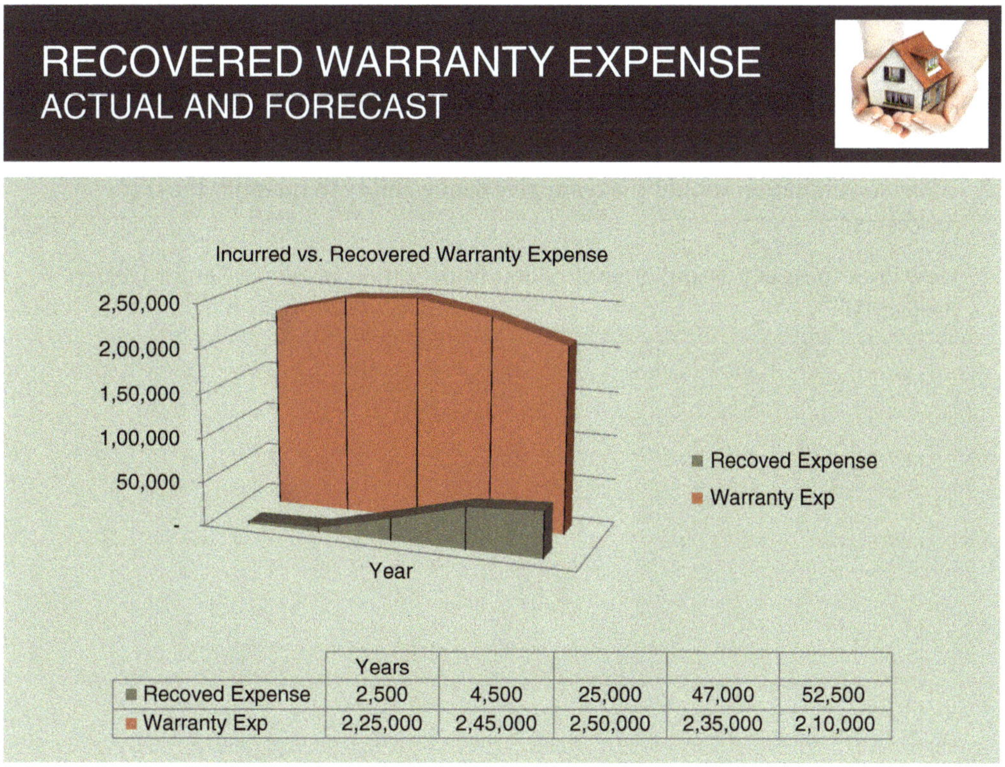

	Years				
Recoved Expense	2,500	4,500	25,000	47,000	52,500
Warranty Exp	2,25,000	2,45,000	2,50,000	2,35,000	2,10,000

• **Figure 2–10** A Graphic Presentation of the Business Case for Change

Looking ahead to the second semester, the team should condense the before and after analysis into a simple graphic. As an example, Figure 2–10 could be used in both Senior Design Project I and in Senior Design Project ll to visually compare the forecasted improvements.

The ability to quantify the As-Is state and, in the next semester, the comparable To-Be state, is the validation of the business case for change. Why would a business manager change a process if there is no problem area in the client's business today or if implementing your solution will not improve the business in the future?

QUESTIONS AND CASE STUDY FOR CHAPTER 2

1. What are the major steps in understanding a client's business for the purpose of evaluating where to focus in the project?
2. What is quantification and why is quantification important in establishing the issues to pursue in a business process?
3. What are the key differences between tangible and intangible evidence in evaluating business processes?
4. What is meant by the term "As-Is" state and why is that state of the business important to the team?

Case Study: A team has documented three processes within their Senior Design Project that are potential areas for detailed analysis and possible improvement. All three processes, if improved, could reduce the time for the processes. The team has determined that they can only focus on one process due to the complexity of the analysis and the allotted time in Senior Design Project I.

1. What would be the deciding factor or factors in making their selection of a process for detailed analysis and potential improve?
2. What consideration should the team give to the ability to quantify the three processes?
3. How does the analysis and quantification impact their results in Senior Design Project II?

CHAPTER 3

Making a Compelling Case for Change

Chapter 3 discusses the analysis of the current, "As-Is," state of the business as the basis for developing ideas to improve the business. These projected improvements will serve as the basis for forecasting the "To-Be" state of the business and represent the compelling case for change.

HIGH-LEVEL SOLUTIONS

Once the team understands (1) the client's operations, (2) the environment of the business, and (3) the area or areas of the business process to be improved, the team can begin to evaluate approaches that can improve the business process. At this point only a high-level set of solutions is required.

In Chapter 2, as part of the discussion on analyzing the business, steps f and g were included as part of the analysis. The steps are repeated here:

a. *Potential High-Level Solutions*—Based on the issues identified, the client, the business environment, and the constraints documented by the team, the team should establish several potential solutions at a high level. These potential solutions will be evaluated in detail during the following semester.
b. *Discuss Analysis with Client*—This step is shown to emphasize that the team should review the business case for change with the client and review the requirements for the high-level solution. Selecting the detailed solution is a topic for Senior Design II.

The solutions are the approaches that have reasonable promise in addressing the business issue. Detailed analysis and selection of the final solution takes place in the second semester. Each project and client will be different but in general teams gravitate to four general types of solutions. The solution categories typically include:

1. A technology solution developed by the team,
2. Implementation of a commercially available package,
3. Implementation of an open source solution, or
4. Some combination of commercial, open source, and team-developed software.

In Senior Design Project I, the objective is to prepare the As-Is Case for Change. The As-Is case, discussed in the previous chapters, represents the current state of the business process under review.

The first approach many teams take is to develop an alternate process for the business areas they determine could be improved. The idea may be to replace several existing processes with a more efficient process using some elements of technology, for example, replacing a paper-based process with a searchable database solution. This replacement approach is indicated in Figure 2–3 from Chapter 2 and repeated here as Figure 3–1.

The challenge to Senior Design Project teams is to consider improvements that may go well beyond the replacement of processes. For example, during the analysis of the business and the competitive environment, the team may suggest a new business avenue to evaluate. This new business avenue might be represented by a revised approach as shown in Figure 3–2.

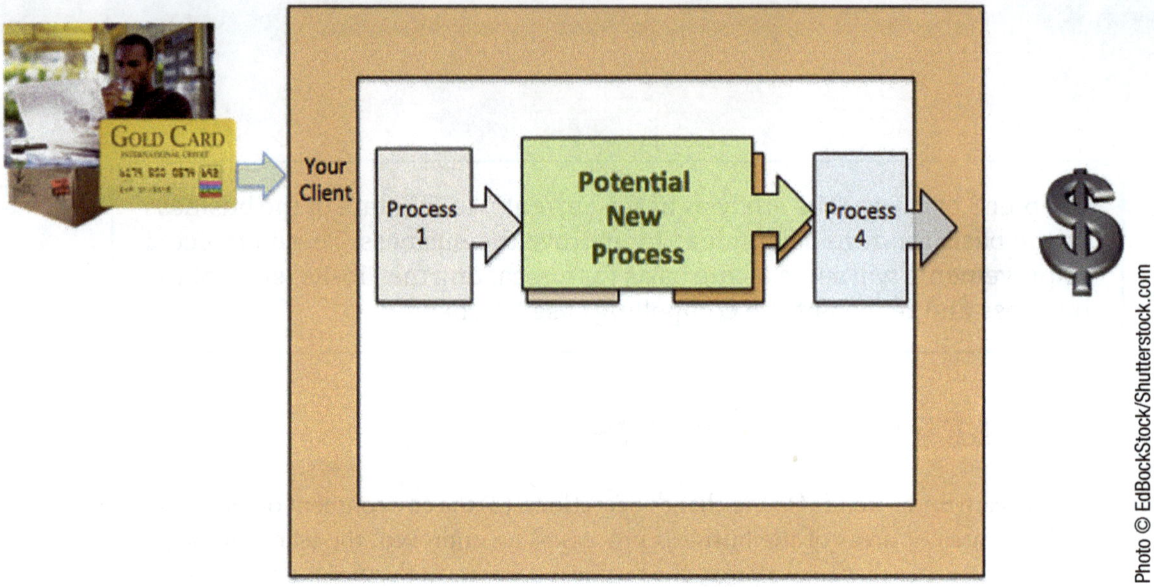

• Figure 3–1 (Repeated from Chapter 2). Step Two: Identifying Areas for Improvement

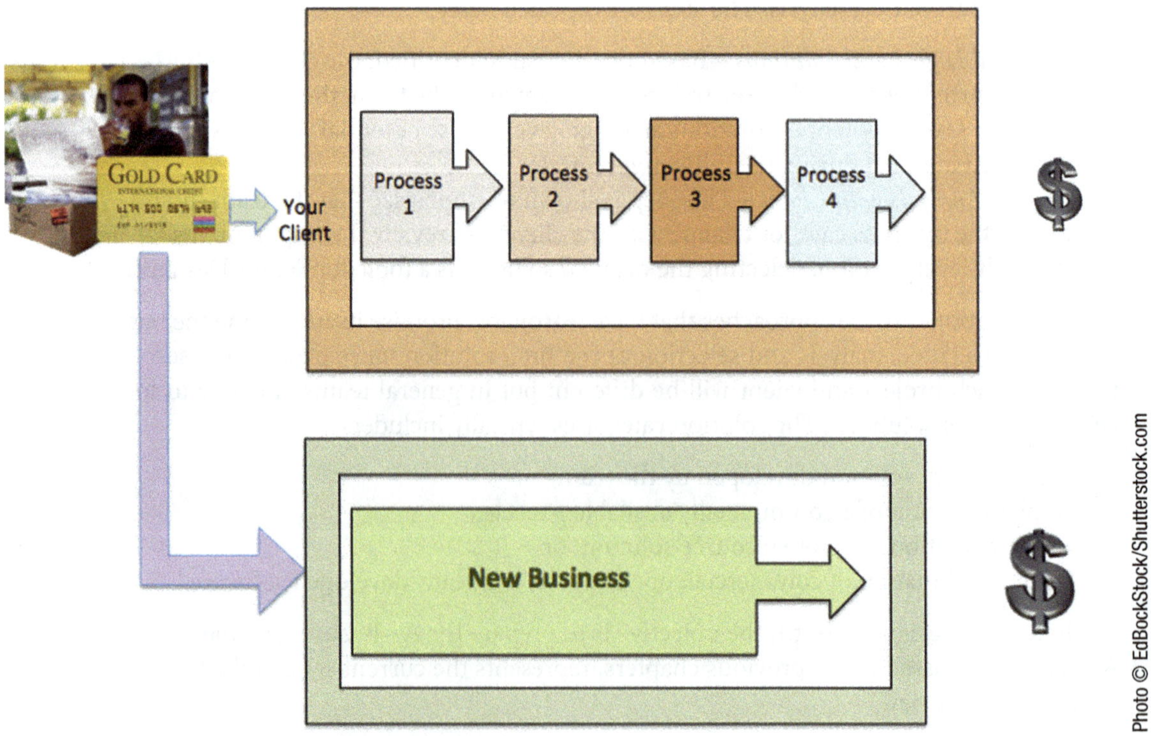

• Figure 3–2 Identifying a Potential New Business

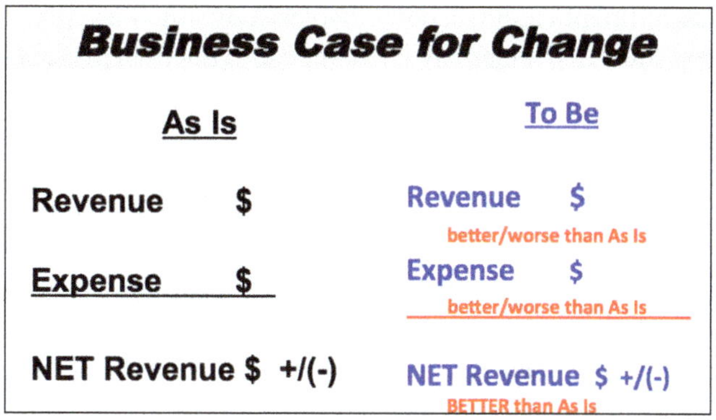

• **Figure 3–3** (repeated from Chapter 2) Business Case for Change Comparison

There are a wide variety of acceptable solutions, solutions that will make a quantifiable improvement in the business. In the earlier analysis carried out in Chapter 2 the team determined the cost of various processes, and now should have identified areas for improvement. These areas could be based on bottlenecks noted in the business or on an understanding of the competitive environment and where this particular business is lacking.

An example of the analysis, quantification, and potential solutions are shown in the sample presentation in Chapter 4 in Figure 4–5, Figure 4–7, and Figure 4–9.

The final step in building the business case for change is to research the potential impact on the business, or rather the impact of the improvement on the business, from implementing the proposed solution. The project will be successful only if the business is improved. The client is unlikely to change processes or enter a new business if there is no benefit to making the change. This forecast of the improved process is the basis for the "To-Be" calculation in this important chart (Figure 3–3).

DEVELOPING THE AS-IS (CURRENT STATE) PRESENTATION

The culminating event of Senior Design Project l is the presentation of the team's analysis to a panel of business leaders. We can now explore the elements the team should address in their presentation. Although the key elements of the presentation are delineated on the scorecard, an important component of this culminating presentation is an orchestration of material that displays the following elements:

1. Demonstrate that you understand the customer's business.
2. Demonstrate that you understand the problem and you can describe the problem.
3. Quantify the problem.
4. Show that you have potential solutions for the problem.
5. Explain items 1, 2, 3, and 4 convincingly within the 15 to 20 minutes allotted.

We will use the Senior Design l scorecard as the template for this discussion. First, we will review the scorecard sections related to the presentation itself. Second, we will review the sections related to content. The presentation delivery accounts for 15% of the total grade. The presentation content accounts for the remaining 85% of the grade.

The scorecard is organized in the logical sequence of a presentation. However, the scorecard sequence is not always the most effective approach in presenting the various elements of a particular client. The objective of the presentation is to demonstrate an effective analysis and solution, as well as be interesting, that is, engaging for the judges and your colleagues.

Based on the assignments identified in Chapter 1, during the semester the members of the team will present most of the elements that appear in the final presentation as individual components. The final presentation requires these individual presentations to be structured into a coherent presentation designed to be convincing. Each team member should script the comments for the particular topics they will cover during the presentation. Unscripted comments should be avoided. The presentation is done within a relatively short time frame, and the likelihood of missing key data is too important to leave to unscripted conversations.

An effective and engaging presentation is a direct result of extensive practice coupled with aggressive editing of themes, revisions of presentation order, supporting messages between presenters, and an effective delivery. The amount of practice and the willingness to make revisions will frequently be the difference between an adequate presentation and an outstanding presentation.

PRESENTATION SCORECARD ELEMENTS

The portion of the scorecard shown below allocates 15% of the results to areas that underpin the presentation with the exception of "Able to answer questions from judges." Several of the scorecard items are quite easy, yet important, and should be straightforward to achieve at least an average grade. However, all the elements require preparation and, therefore, require planning. The team can use the draft presentation as a complete dress rehearsal of all these elements.

Presentation is Clear	0	6	7	8	9	10
Effective use of visual media						
Media and presentation are consistent and clear						

Team is Convincing	0	1	2	3	4	5
Demonstrates enthusiasm and conviction						
Able to answer questions from judges						

One of the elements being graded is the effective use of presentation material. The team is not limited to presenting slides as the sole medium. Use of multimedia elements can be quite effective. There are numerous sources to help the student team understand what makes an effective and engaging presentation. Teams are encouraged to review outside resources and practice their presentation before they are scheduled to deliver the finished presentation.

CONTENT SCORECARD ELEMENTS

There are six elements to be addressed in the content portion of the presentation. These elements and their maximum score per element are:

1. Enterprise Described – 10 points of total grade
2. Business Process Described and Quantified – 30 points of total grade
3. What Can Be Improved by IT – 15 points of total grade
4. Proposed Solution – 15 points of total grade
5. Implementation Challenges – 15 points of total grade

The most heavily weighted items are (1) the business process described (the As-Is state of the business) and (2) the compelling case for change. Both of these elements come from the analysis leading to the quantification of the business problem. Many business components can be quantified, but a select few will be such a serious issue that modifying the process will yield a significant improvement in the business and therefore worthy of a concerted effort to quantify the process.

The analysis described in Chapters 1 and 2 generate the details for this content. However, the analysis does not provide a method for integrating the completed analysis into an effective presentation.

One method is to construct the presentation allocating time to the six elements from the scorecard based on using three presentation slides for the more heavily weighted items and using two presentation slides for the other four sections. Then determine the overall theme and the most compelling approach to describe the compelling business case. Once presentation slides have been allocated to a portion of the presentation, then develop the message for each presentation element and each speaker. This process will generate the beginning of a presentation.

With the basic elements of content as placeholders, the team should array the information in a manner that would convey a continuous theme where the basics are laid out and then validated with research and details. This would be true for the elements of the business environment, the problem and its impact, and last, the area of potential solutions. In many cases, a graphic representation of the business flow would be most effective in conveying the essence of a business.

The last portion of preparation for the presentation is to determine which summary facts will adequately convey the research and conclusions developed by the team, and which facts will be supporting documents to clarify questions from the judges. The team should also determine who will field questions, and who is best at answering questions based on their role in developing the presentation.

The content scorecard, the current version is shown below, should be used to measure the completeness of the business portion of the presentation, but not necessarily as a detailed agenda for the presentation.

Business and Competition	0	6	7	8	9	10
Enterprise business described Industry, Services, Ownership, Size, P&L, History Complexity of Business						

Processes Described and Quantified	0	18	21	24	27	30
Business Process Described Process Quantified ($, personnel, time, eqmt) Compelling Business Case for Change explained						

What Can Be Improved by IT	0	7	9	11	13	15
Has entire AS-IS Process been considered Solution Requirements Described Issues of all four Concentrations identified						

Proposed Solutions	0	7	9	11	13	15
Multiple solutions have been considered What elements of IT might be used Generic description of the TO-BE process Solutions are technically sophisticated and innovative						

Implementation Challenges	0	7	9	11	13	15
Business culture challenges Financial, Time, People, Training, Sustainment Client Acceptance Criteria Described 493 Development and Implementation Schedule						

QUESTIONS AND CASE STUDY FOR CHAPTER 3

1. What does the phrase "business case for change" mean when looking at a team's Senior Design Project?
2. In the final presentation of the semester, which elements are weighted most heavily on the scorecard? How do these weights influence the presentation content?
3. The As-Is state depicts the current processes and costs of the client's business. What information could be used to forecast the To-Be state?

Case Study: The team has identified a particular process to improve in the client's business. There are two solutions that could be suggested to the client. One is a custom solution to be built by the team during Senior Design Project II. A second solution is a commercially available solution. The team would prefer to build the custom solution for the experience they would gain.

1. What factors might be considered in comparing the two solutions? The discussion might compare the pros and cons of the two approaches. For example, one factor to consider may be how well the two solutions fit the client's particular processes. A custom-built solution would closely match the client's needs. With a commercial solution, the client's processes would have to adhere to the predefined solution.
2. How would the selection of a team-built solution change the team's schedule in the following semester?
3. In discussing the two solutions with the client what issues might concern the client? As one idea, would the client need an IT support team in house to maintain the team-built solution?

CHAPTER

4 Sample As-Is (Current State) Presentation

Chapter 4 is an example of a complete first semester presentation. Each presentation element, having been developed using techniques described in Chapters 1, 2, and 3, is combined to present the client's business and the suggested areas for improvement. The presentation included in this chapter is quite basic, and the example is included only as a starting point for a complete presentation.

A sample of a final presentation of Senior Design Project I, the first of the two semesters, is an effective way to understand the effort required from the student teams. This chapter will examine a generic presentation for Senior Design Project I. The presentation included in this workbook is merely intended to show the basic elements that teams typically include in an end-of-semester presentation. Teams are expected to far exceed this basic sample presentation, including more comprehensive descriptions, enhanced graphics, and photographic or video material, providing the reviewers with a comprehensive and compelling demonstration of the current state of the client business and processes.

It should be noted that static presentations, such as the one included in this chapter, are only the infrastructure for the presenting team. The script that the team members add to the static material is crucial to an effective and engaging presentation. There are many sources available to the students that provide guidance on developing effective speaking points to enhance the overall presentation, and within the course itself significant time and guidance is provided to prepare the students for oral presentations.

SAMPLE AS-IS (CURRENT STATE) PRESENTATION

Although the presentation in this chapter represents a concluding presentation from the first semester, students are encouraged to review the generic presentation in Part II of the workbook as well to see the culmination of both semesters of work. The reason for encouraging the reader to study the concluding presentation is to provide an insight into the entire capstone effort. Reviewing the final solution will allow the student team to focus on elements that will carry over from the first semester to second semester. It should provide a roadmap that avoids unnecessary detours and, therefore, unnecessary rework.

In most cases, only a few presentation elements from Senior Design l will be included in the second semester presentation. This limited reuse refers only to the actual material presented at the end of the second semester, not to the analysis and supporting documentation developed during the first semester of work. There are several reasons which limit reuse of the first semester material. The first reason is the time constraint of presenting a much more complete view of the solution in Senior Design Project II, not just the business situation. Second, the intent in the second semester is significantly different, with a focus on the development and implementation of a solution and its positive impact on the business. One component that will be addressed in both the first semester presentation and the second semester is the quantification of the solution's impact. This is discussed in Chapters 3 and 6 of the workbook.

In the following presentation, there will be examples of the various presentation elements that examine specific key items to be included in first semester presentation. But we will begin with the complete generic presentation representing the culmination of Senior Design Project I.

Because the workbook is limited to a static presentation, it is necessary to provide some context to the generic presentation in this chapter. Although this particular example is a non-profit organization, the elements that must be addressed by the student team in course of the Senior Design Projects I and II are similar to those that would be examined in a for-profit business. As background, the business under review is a non-profit, charitable organization that provides short-term housing for families, as well as home ownership education. The organization supports its efforts through contributions and fundraising from individuals and corporations using online and direct mail solicitations. Their housing portfolio is comprised of 150 single-family, townhouse, and condominium properties located in a suburban metropolitan area.

For brevity, several basic slides have been omitted. These include a presentation agenda, pictures of team members, and a concluding slide. In the formal presentation, all team members are identified including a picture of each member and their role on the team.

The static elements of a Senior Design Project l presentation are shown in Figure 4–1 through Figure 4–10 with brief explanatory comments. These are in a typical sequence of the presentation but this sequence is not a requirement. Each team should determine the sequence that most clearly describes their client, analysis and solution.

In order to better depict the business case and the areas to be improved, most presentations will include a graphic presentation of the business areas' current state. With limited time to provide a comprehensive presentation, a relatively simple graphic depiction is an effective way to help the judges understand the business case being developed and presented by the team.

Recall that this presentation is suggestive of a presentation made at the end of the first semester. As the team moves into the selection and implementation of a solution in the second semester, previously undiscovered challenges may appear.

This example of a final Senior Design Project l presentation is not intended to be the outline for future presentations. Each client, each team, and each project will have unique elements and presentation strategies. Teams will usually add a view of their schedule, more depth on the business organization, and significantly more details on the quantification of the business process under review. However, this sample does touch on many of the important elements that should be discussed in a complete presentation at the conclusion of Senior Design Project l.

• **Figure 4–1** Introduction—This is an introductory slide and is typically followed by team pictures. Many teams use the company logo or other identifying material.

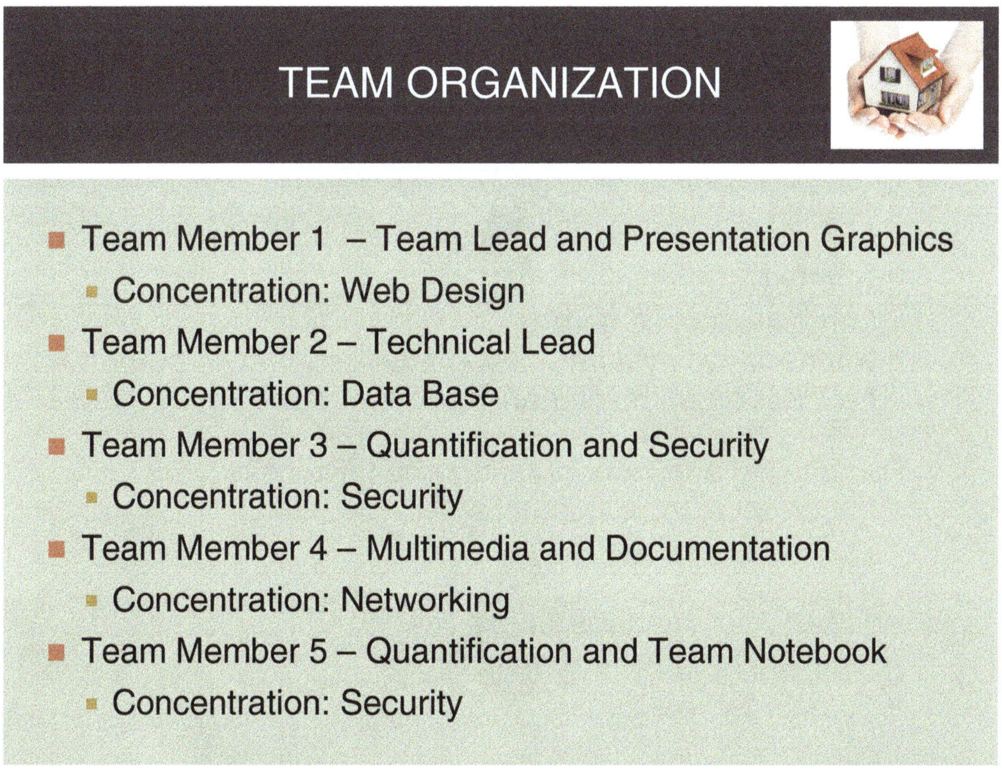

• **Figure 4–2** Team Organization—The team's duties may evolve during the first semester and will change significantly as the requirements of the second semester are understood.

CONTEXT OF BUSINESS

- Home Until Home, Inc. is a non-profit organization recognized under IRS code as a 501(c)3 charitable organization.
- Mission: Provide a stable housing environment for families in need within our community.
- Assets include 150 single-family houses and townhouses.
- Full time staff of 25 and approximately 100 volunteers.
- Funding from community grants, corporate donations, and individual donations. Solicitation by email and direct mail.
- Annual budget of approximately $19 million
  - $ 2.5 million - staff salaries and benefits
  - $ 10.0 million - property maintenance, utilities, and household goods
  - $ 1.5 million - fundraising and donor support
  - $ 5.0 million - property purchase, rent, subsidies, and other expenses

• **Figure 4–3** Context of Business—This slide is a summary of the business and begins to establish the parameters of the business' environment and establishes the broad parameters of the as-is, that is, the current state.

KEY BUSINESS PROCESSES

- Property Maintenance
  - Largest expense item
  - Paper based system – 3 ring binders for each property
  - No tracking of maintenance costs or timing
- Fundraising and Donor Management Process
  - Important external relations
  - No online payment process
- Housing Assignment Process
- Accounting and Bill Payment Process
- Volunteer Scheduling

• **Figure 4–4** Key Business Processes—An important slide that entails a simple and direct explanation of the processes involved in this business. This slide coincides with the more significant annual budget items shown on Figure 4–3.

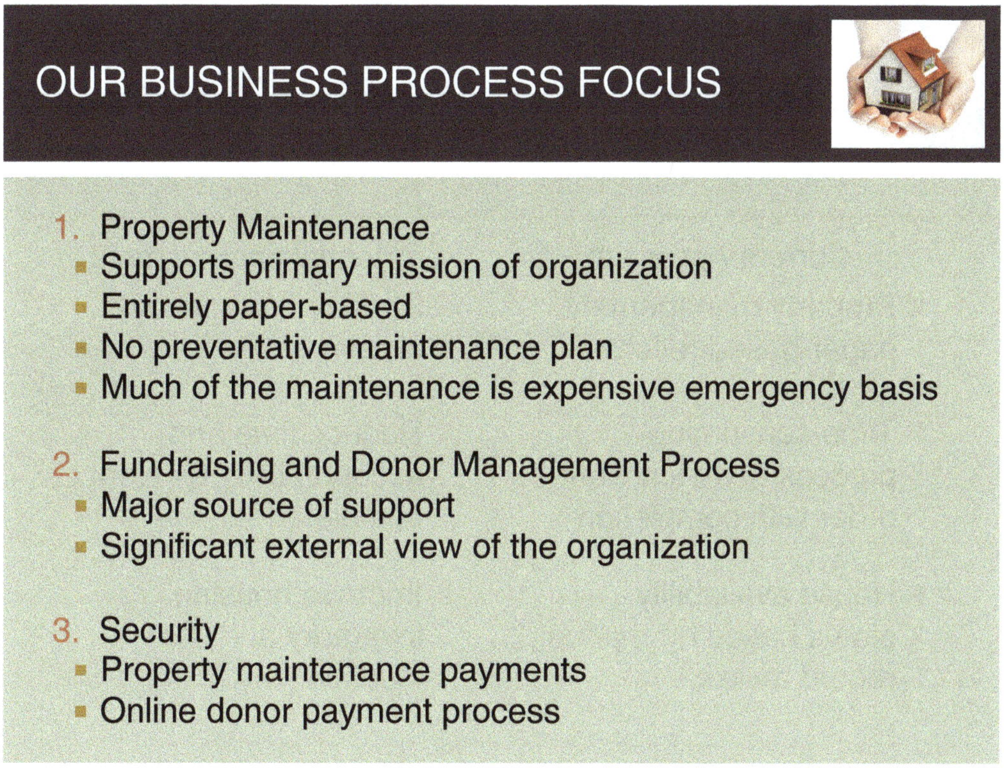

● **Figure 4–5** Our Business Process Focus—The slide is unambiguous as to the focus of the team's analysis and future resolution. The slide describes why these problems exist, and why they are rewarding areas for the company to invest time and effort to improve.

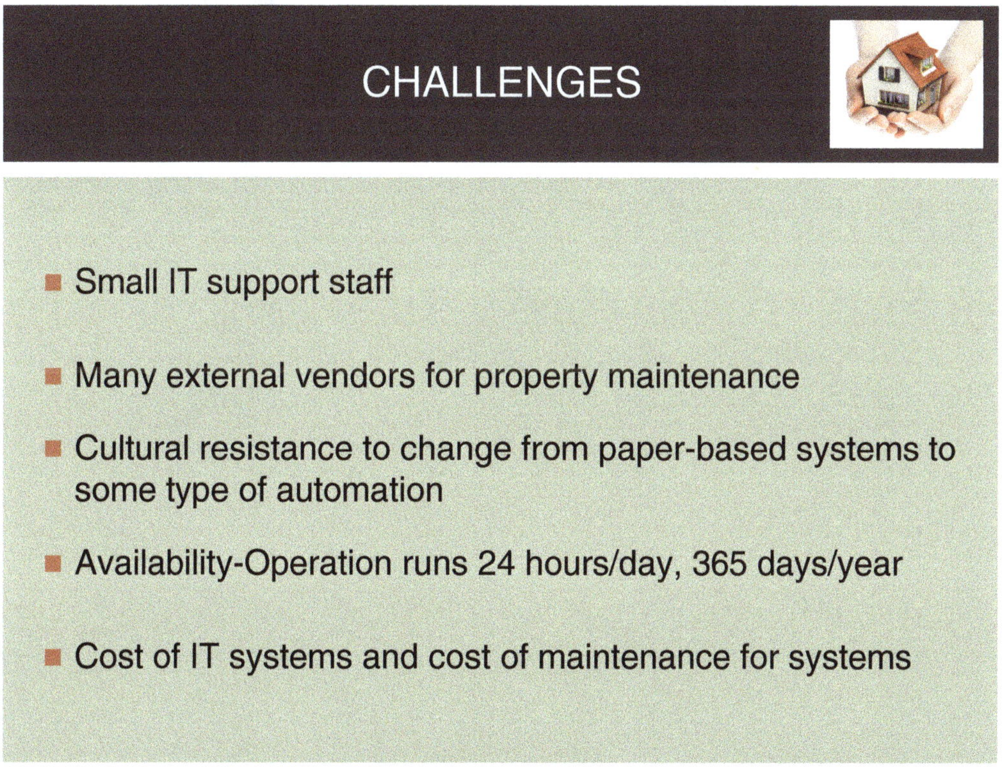

● **Figure 4–6** Challenges—Business situations typically have a variety of influences supporting or opposing potential changes to existing business processes. These influences may be internal, such as a culture that resists changes, or external, like loss of additional business from clients accustomed to the current process. This slide describes those key challenges.

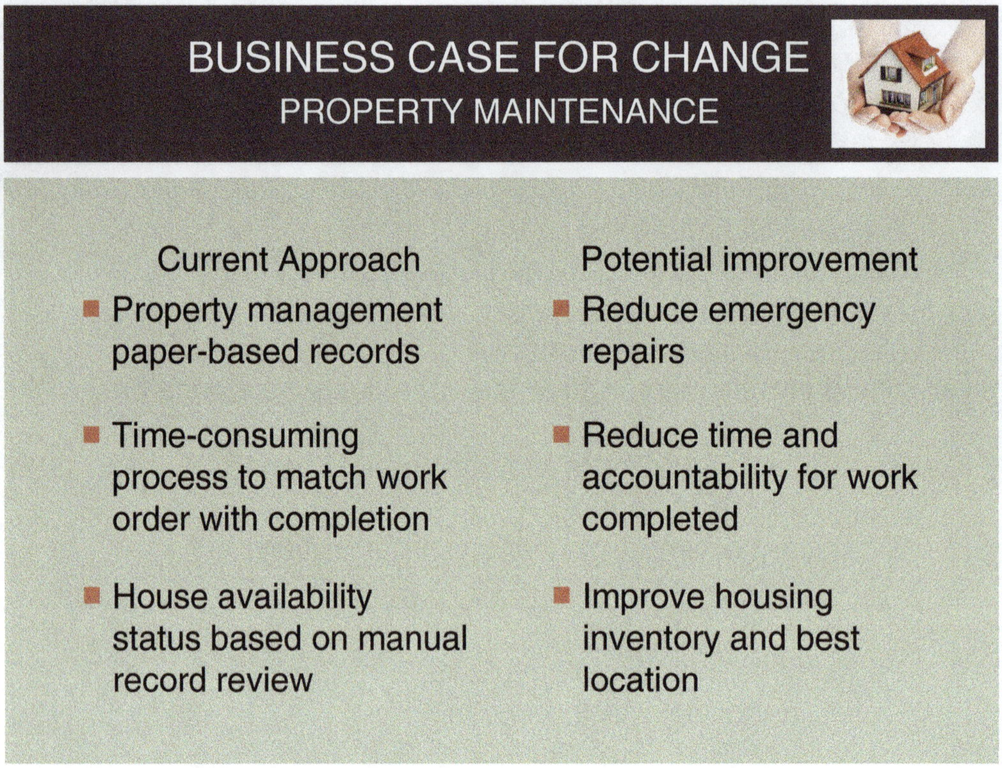

Figure 4–7 Business Case for Change—Property Maintenance—This slide represents only one of the three business process areas identified in earlier slides. The remaining two areas are not shown in this example but will be discussed in Part II of the workbook. The information displayed and discussed by the presenting team compares the current business process (shown on the right of the slide) to the potential improvements (shown on the left). This slide introduces the processes that the team will evaluate quantitatively, those that will be improved, and, in Part II, will be re-measured. The process of quantifying the business process was described in Chapter 2.

QUANTIFICATION
PROPERTY MAINTENANCE

Current Approach	Current Cost
Entering data – two full-time staff	Annual cost = $21,500 each for $43,000
Reporting – 50% staff	Annual cost = $10,500
Emergency maintenance premium	Estimated by client to be 5–8% of maintenance or approx $250,000

Figure 4–8 Quantification—This slide is the topic of Chapters 2 and 3 and is included here to maintain the flow of a typical presentation. This slide represents only one of the three business process areas identified in earlier slides. The remaining two areas are not shown in this example but will be shown in Part II of the workbook.

POSSIBLE SOLUTIONS

1. Property Maintenance
   - Commercial or open source PC database system
   - Implement a simple Visual Basic/Excel based tracking system
   - Outsource maintenance entirely
2. Fundraising and Donor Management Process
   - Commercial or open source PC CRM system
   - Implement a simple Visual Basic/Excel based tracking system
   - Outsource payment collection and processing
3. Security
   - Complete security audit
   - Focus on shortfalls in property maintenance system and online donor payment process
   - Institute backup plans for critical systems like property management

Figure 4–9 Possible Solutions—Since the focus of the first semester is to understand the business environment of the client, only high-level solutions are required in the first semester. These solutions, which the team has vetted with the client, are avenues of research during the second semester. This was the subject of Chapter 3 and also Part II of the workbook.

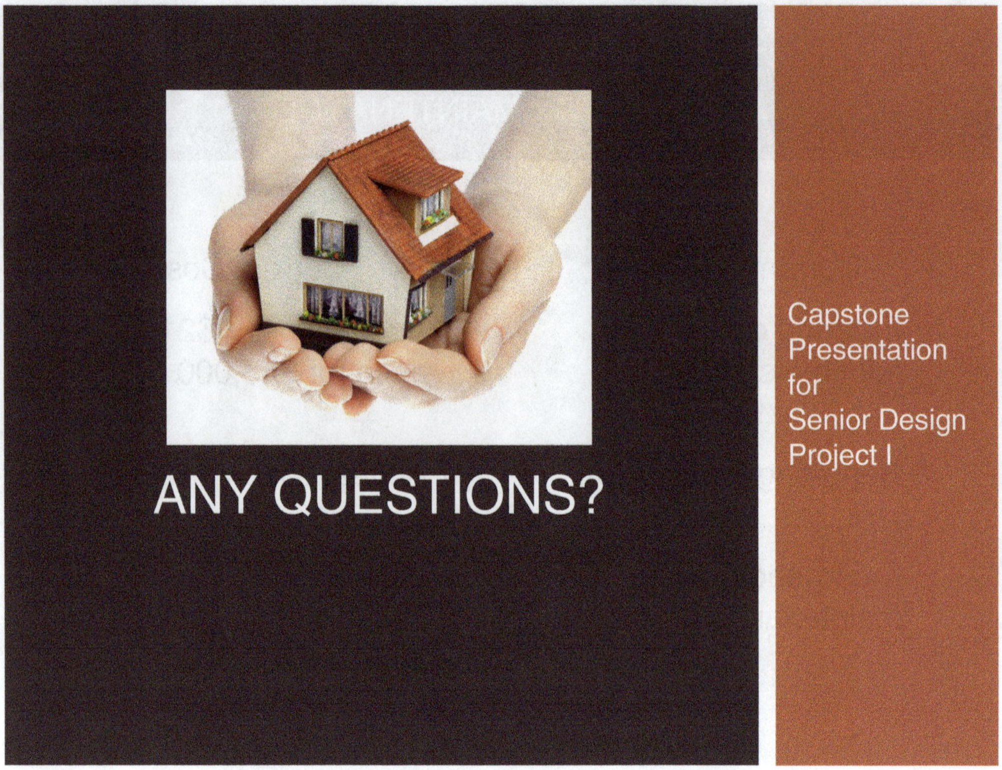

● **Figure 4–10** Conclusion—The team typically invites questions. An alternative is to show a conclusion that summarizes their strongest or most interesting elements. The team could leave these key points of interest as their final slide of the presentation, and potentially as an aid in answering questions from the judging panel. Some teams have ended with a short video showing some component of their suggested improvement.

THE SEMESTER-ENDING PRESENTATION AS A BUILDING BLOCK

The analysis completed in the first semester provides the team with a critical basis for moving into the following semester's effort. The team has established the following tasks:

1. *Selection of the Business Client and Project*—Both the client and the client's particular issues will be clearly established.
2. *Client Relations*—The team and the client have established a norm for interaction and discussion. The ability to communicate with the client will be important as the team moves into the next semester.
3. *Client Business Environment*—The team has a clear view into the client's business and the business environment, typically areas that are new to most, if not all, of the team members. The environment may limit the choices for an effective solution to the business problem.
4. *Documentation of Business Processes*—The current business processes of the client business have been studied and documented.
5. *Current (As-Is) State*—An understanding of the current business processes has been established as well as a broader understanding of the overall business in relation to the processes under analysis.

tification—The current business issues have been established and measured in ·ary terms as a basis for measuring the future improvements. The method for ·ing the current process, which will be repeated in the second semester, has ·cumented.

' High-Level Solutions—Based on the problem, the client, the business ·ent, and the constraints, three potential solutions have been developed and to the client. These potential solutions will be evaluated during the second

' OUT SENIOR DESIGN PROJECT PART I

·r at the end of Senior Design Project l that will be important as the team ·o Senior Design Project ll.

·ty is to incorporate the feedback from the judges during the final ·ges' questions are an indication of areas that were not clearly explained. Design Project l final presentation will be consolidated into a small ·ation materiel for use in Senior Design Project ll. Updating these the presentation and should help the team avoid having to rework ·he following semester.

· is to provide feedback to the client on the final presentation. · a bridge during the period between semesters where the team's · is normally minimal.

·D CASE STUDY FOR CHAPTER 4

·nts might be used in addition to the team's final pre- ·ight these elements be most effective during the

·ight be added to the sample presentation in this chapter ·entation?

·esentation would you share with the client and for

·ase Study: You are a reviewer, not a presenter, of the sample presentation in this chapter. Using the information in Chapters 2 and 3, discuss the following:

1. What was the "business case for change" in the presentation?
2. What process or processes were analyzed and quantified to show the As-Is state?
3. Is the quantification based on tangible evidence or intangible evidence?

PART II

Developing the Solution

CHAPTER

5 Organize for a Successful Solution

Chapter 5 focuses on the planning, development, and implementation of the client solution. Planning is critical because of the amount of effort required to select, build, implement, and train the client. In addition to interaction with the client, the team needs to prepare presentations on the individual assignments.

TEAM ORGANIZATION FOR SENIOR DESIGN PROJECT II

The start of the second semester is an excellent time to review the team infrastructure, meeting frequency, team leadership, team organization, and assignments. The team has had the benefit of working together over the previous semester and should discuss changes that will improve team effectiveness. Teams are encouraged to change team leadership for the second semester to a member with strong project management skills. This semester is focused on development and implementation, which is an operational set of tasks. This is different than the project in the former semester, which was focused on a more abstract effort of understanding the business.

The efforts for Senior Design Project ll will complete the process of transforming the identified business problem into a resolved business process. The learning objectives remain consistent with those presented in Senior Design Project l. These learning objectives are as follows:

1. Learn how to plan for and manage the delivery of a successful meeting.
2. Learn how to quantify the challenges presented by a business process.
3. Learn how to identify unfulfilled opportunities and benefits caused by a process challenge.
4. Learn how to engage an audience in planning for and delivering effective sales and situation briefings and presentations.
5. Develop an effective management team.
6. Understand the importance of leading peers to create an effective team.

It is generally anticipated that the work effort involved in Senior Design Project ll is not only significant, but surpasses that of Senior Design Project I. This increased effort is due to three factors. First, the team's effort turns from primarily researching a business issue to that of "selling" the improvement to the client, developing the solution, and implementing the solution. Second, the team must fashion an evaluation of the solution that provides evidence that the business process has been changed for the better. Third, the team has to document, train, implement, and demonstrate their actual solution.

In Chapter 7 we will review the scorecard for Senior Design Project ll for a more complete perspective on the final presentation. Since the focus of this second semester course is on developing and implementing a solution, the scorecard topics and weights are significantly different than those shown in Chapter 3 for Senior Design Project I.

As the team approaches this second semester, it is critical to manage interactions with the client. As mentioned earlier, client contact between semesters will foster a continuing working relationship with the client. To set the expectations for the client for the second semester, the team must first set their own expectations. The approach best suited to establish this expectation is a schedule including key milestones and deliverables.

In Chapter 1 we discussed a generic project diagram, including the elements of planning, initializing, and building the business case for change. Looking at this generic project as related to Senior Design Project ll, the major components are selection, plan, build, install and turn over. The steps can be summarized in Figure 5-1.

The primary activities in applying the generic project steps to Senior Design Project ll are as follows:

Select Solution—The team has to select a solution from the high-level solutions proposed in Senior Design I, design all the elements of a complete solution, and determine the necessary client infrastructure to successfully implement the solution. The solution to be built is based on the evaluation of alternatives discussed in Senior Design Project l and modified based on feedback from the client and the first semester presentation.

Plan— The team should develop a work breakdown structure (WBS) that includes all the steps needed to complete the project. The WBS should also include sufficient time to prepare and practice for the final presentation of the project. A sample WBS is included later in the chapter.

Build, Test, and Document— During this effort the team should build, integrate, and populate the solution as needed. The team must also measure the impact of their solution by replicating the measurements used to quantify the As-Is condition. The team should also calculate the return on investment (ROI) for the improved process and application. Testing may involve both team members and client staff members. Documentation should be provided to the client describing the solution, any warranty available, and vendor points of contact. Unlike an in-house development team, the student team will not be available to support the solution.

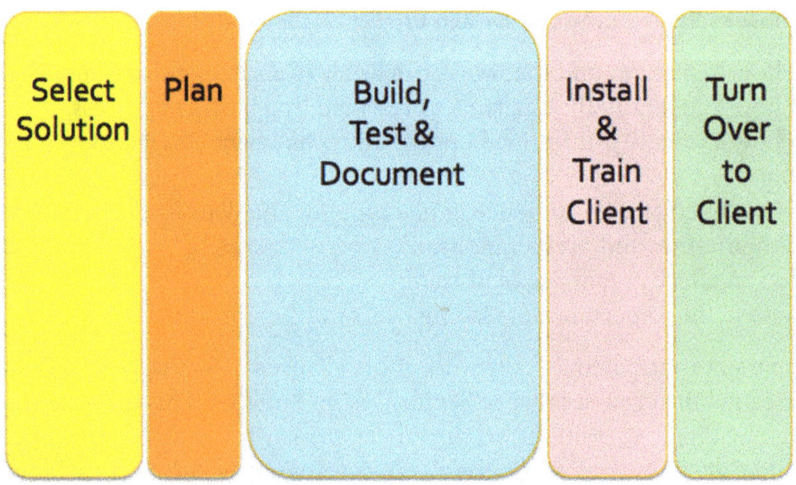

• Figure 5–1 General Project Activities

Install and Train Client—The team needs to install the solution at the client site and provide training and documentation.

Turn Over to Client— The client's acceptance of the solution is the conclusion of the project. The team should provide a set of documents to the client including descriptions of hardware and software requirements, maintenance agreements, warranties, points of contact at the vendors, and a copy of code developed by the team.

PREPARING THE SCHEDULE

The team will develop a schedule for the semester in order to move from the generic project plan discussed above to a successfully completed project. This schedule, as compared to the schedule developed in Senior Design Project l, will have more tasks and be delineated in more detail since more of the tasks will have significant dependencies and short time frames. The schedule should be established during the first week of the semester

At the conclusion of Senior Design Project l, as discussed in Chapters 3 and 4, the team proposed several possible solutions. Going from several possible solutions to a finished project requires numerous steps:

1. Evaluation of alternate solutions
2. Selection of a preferred solution
3. Agreement with client on solution
4. Software design and documentation
5. Development of components (software, database, and web)
6. Implementation plan
7. Training plan
8. Testing plan
9. Documentation of component solutions and training material
10. Implementation in a test environment or the client location
11. Testing
12. Quantification of the implemented solution
13. Turnover and client acceptance
14. Preparation of the various status presentations and the final presentation.

To accomplish all these steps, all of which would be included in a typical information technology project, the team should build two *detailed* schedules. The first schedule will be the project schedule, that is, from the date of the first team meeting of the semester to the date of draft presentation. The second schedule is the presentation schedule.

For the semester project schedule it is best to work backwards from the date of the draft presentation, with a target to complete development, implementation, turnover, and quantification of the project in sufficient time to incorporate the results into the draft presentation. Validate the schedule with the instructor and the client, and use this as the baseline project schedule. This is one of the assignments discussed in Chapter 6.

The second schedule is the presentation schedule, the allocation of the 15 to 20 minutes allocated for the team to make the final presentation to the judges. This presentation schedule will be the allocation of time to the elements that effectively present the business and solution. A sample schedule for the presentation is not included but a completed generic presentation is included in Chapter 7, which may serve as a basis for your presentation schedule.

SAMPLE PROJECT SCHEDULE

In establishing the project schedule, work back from the date of the draft presentation, not the final presentation. The time between the draft presentation and the final presentation should be dedicated only to revising, tuning, and practicing the end-of-semester presentation.

The sample schedule included below for Senior Design Project II shows the number of steps needed to accomplish these tasks. A significant risk factor in completing the project within the time horizon is that much of the effort is completed during the later part of the semester with little time to recover from a misstep. The schedule shown does not include key milestones. This will come from your class activities, due dates for class assignments, and from discussions with your client.

As an example of the time constraints, the quantification of the revised business process occurs near the end of the WBS, shown as step 14. If the results are not measurable or do not generate the anticipated saving, there is little time for an alternate approach. This is not to say that the schedule should change. Rather, it indicates that sufficient time needs to be set aside to accomplish a thorough evaluation, and that time cannot be slighted. Some of the early major tasks include a few suggested subtasks.

Senior Design Project II Sample Schedule		
1.0	**Prior Semester Presentation**	
2.0	**Develop Work Plan**	
	2.1	Develop Work Breakdown Structure
	2.2	Develop Project Staffing Plan
	2.3	Develop Project Schedule
	2.4	Develop Project Budget
3.0	**Evaluation of Alternate Solutions**	
	3.1	Research Alternatives
	3.2	Develop Ranking method
	3.3	Team Meeting to rank and select solution
	3.4	Document Team Meeting
4.0	**Create Beta Solution**	
	4.1	Design Beta Solution
	4.2	Code or Buy Software Components
	4.3	Implement in Test Facility
	4.4	Evaluate Beta Solution
	4.5	Revise Solution
5.0	**Team Status Presentation**	
6.0	**Meeting with Client**	
	6.1	Prepare Agenda and Material
	6.2	Present Beta solution
	6.3	Discuss feedback and revisions

Senior Design Project II Sample Schedule		
	6.4	Agree in Solution elements
	6.5	Discuss Project Timeline and Solution Delivery
	6.6	Document Client Meeting
7.0	**Software design and documentation**	
8.0	**Development of components**	
	8.1	Acquire Hardware Platform
	8.2	Design and Develop Software Components
	8.3	Design and Develop Database Components
	8.4	Design and Develop Web Components
9.0	**Development of Solution Plans**	
	9.1	Develop and Document Implementation Plan
	9.2	Develop and Document Security Plan
	9.3	Develop and Document Training Plan
	9.4	Develop and Document Testing Plan
10.0	**Team Status Presentation**	
11.0	**Documentation of Solution and Training Material**	
12.0	**Implementation in Test Environment**	
13.0	**Testing**	
14.0	**Quantification of Revised Business Process**	
15.0	**Team Status Presentation**	
16.0	**Training**	
17.0	**Turnover and Client Acceptance**	
18.0	**In-Class Demonstration**	
19.0	**Prepare and Present Draft Presentation**	
20.0	**Complete Team Notebook**	
21.0	**Prepare and Present Final Presentation**	

Chapter 6 discusses selection of the final solution but you can see that there is a significant effort to start from two or three potential solutions to arrive at a developed, implemented, and documented final solution. This process will be the discussion covered in Chapters 6 and 7.

QUESTIONS AND CASE STUDY FOR CHAPTER 5

1. What organizational elements of the team should be considered as you start Senior Design Project II?
2. What are the general project activities for Senior Design Project II?
3. In building the team's schedule for the semester, in addition to the list of tasks, what elements could be included?

Case Study: A team in Senior Design Project I developed a preliminary schedule for this second semester as part of their final semester presentation last semester. At the start of this semester the team developed a detailed schedule for Senior Design Project II encompassing 98 calendar days. This forecast includes the day of the final presentation.
In spite of their efforts the team is approximately 5 days behind schedule at the midpoint of the semester. The team's final presentation date cannot be moved.

1. What elements of the schedule or project should the team evaluate?
2. Who should be informed of the schedule slippage?
3. What information should the team provide to each person or group they plan to inform?

CHAPTER

6 Elements of a Complete Solution

Chapter 6 details the selection and implementation steps necessary for the team to accomplish and document a successful senior design project. The set of assignments provides the building blocks for a completed project. Chapter 6 also reviews the scorecard for the final presentation of the semester.

ELEMENTS OF A COMPLETE PROJECT

This second semester focuses on developing and implementing a business process improvement or a change in business infrastructure as discussed in Chapters 2 and 3. Success requires a significant expansion of the analysis completed in the first semester. The new elements that must be accomplished and incorporated into the finished project and the final presentation include:

- Selecting a suitable solution for the issue identified
- Convincing the client of the solution
- Developing and implementing the solution
- Documenting the solution
- Training the client
- Measuring the effects of the solution on the process

In the assignments and the final presentation the team must provide evidence that they provided a positive impact for the client. This evidence is typically shown by discussion of the following tasks in the final presentation. These presentation tasks mirror the scorecard used by the judges during the final presentation:

Original Business Process Described (from prior semester):

- Business Environment and Workflow Described.
- Quantification of Problem is Clear.
- Compelling Business Case for Change Explained.

IT Solution:

- Alternatives Evaluated and Selection Process is coherent.
- The IT Solution is Clearly Described.
- The IT solution addresses the major problem(s).
- Network Security is Properly Addressed.
- The IT solution includes an innovative solution.
- The IT solution is challenging.

Original Business Process Changed:
- Changes to the original business workflow described.
- Economic impact of IT solution explained (To Be vs. As Is).
- Quantification is based on Supportable Evidence.

Business Problem Solved:
- Entire As-Is Business Process Considered.
- Challenges to implementation addressed and resolved.
- IA and Network Security issues analyzed and resolved.

Solution Implemented:
- Project is Finished.
- Comprehensive Testing is Demonstrated.
- Implementation is Complete and Accepted by Client.
- Documentation is Complete and Provided.
- Training and Training Documentation is Complete.
- IT Solution Sustainment is Addressed.
- The Solution is Demonstrated.

Selecting a suitable solution—At the conclusion of the first semester the team proposed several high-level solutions that could provide a positive impact to the client business. The team must devise a method to quickly evaluate these alternatives and potentially new ones based on additional research completed since the first semester. These must be evaluated from the perspective of their impact on the business process, their acceptance by the client, and critically important, by the team's ability to implement the solution within the time constraints of the semester. The project solution may necessitate a reduction in the scope of the project to fit into the time frame of the course.

Convincing the client of the solution—Client acceptance is a significant milestone in a project. If the proper elements were analyzed and a compelling case for changing the process was established with the client, the last step is to convince the client of the suitability of the solution the team is proposing to implement. This exercise is a parallel to what will be in the final presentation.

Developing and implementing the solution—The effort to design, develop, and implement the solution will be the most time-consuming part of the project. The steps involved should follow one of the established development lifecycles rather than be attempted on an ad hoc basis. A clear set of milestones and deliverables in concert with the time allotted will provide the team a number of check points to evaluate their progress. This is an area where additional help from the faculty may be needed. The team should schedule adequate checkpoints to ensure that assistance from the faculty or other teams is requested in a timely manner.

Documenting the solution—Following an established lifecycle will provide for design and development documentation, including test procedures and data conversion schemas for the project. System design and coding documents should be shared with the client and be included in the project notebook prepared by the team.

Training for the client—The team will develop a training strategy for the client. This may be a custom-developed video or training provided by a commercial company. In many cases, the team will provide the initial training to the client.

Measuring the effects of the solution—The final element to be evaluated by the team is the effectiveness of their solution. In the first semester the team measured the existing client system in the process of quantifying the extent of the problem. This was discussed in Chapter 2. The team must measure the newly implemented process and take comparable measurements to ensure the system has improved.

Directly comparable measurements are often difficult to secure since in many cases the time constraints on the team will not be adequate to implement the improvement, train the client, and then have enough cycles using the improved processes to provide reliable data.

As an alternative, research on the effects of similar improvements may suffice. Reasonable assumptions, clearly identified, may be necessary to tie the researched data to the client project. This alternative approach may take significant research. Time for this task should be in the team's schedule.

ASSIGNMENTS —THE BUILDING BLOCKS

The assignments for Senior Design II build the documentation and also provide the material for the final presentation. Each project will be unique, so only general guidance as to content is provided. Discussions with the faculty will help the team members develop the deliverables.

Due to the time constraints in the semester, teams should focus on developing and documenting a complete package of their results as they process through the semester in order to avoid duplicate work, or work accumulating until the end of the semester. The individual deliverables should be assigned to various team members as the responsible person. Coordination of the individual deliverables is critical so the overall set complements each individual component.

Figure 6-1 shows the relationship between the activities, the documentation, and the notebook the team is building as evidence of their semester efforts.

The particular components of these documents are suggested in each assignment. In many cases the assignments pose a question as a guide to help fashion the response rather than a definitive statement. Each project will be different but the assignments should be written with the goal of using the deliverable in the notebook with only minor revisions. The following is a list of the individual assignments and related descriptions or questions to be addressed in the narrative.

Assignment 1. Project Plan: Team Lead

- Why are you doing this project?
- Who is responsible for what?
- What resources are required?
- How much time should be allocated for each major task?
- Where will the project be carried out?
- Project GANTT chart with milestones.

Assignment 2. Development Plan

- Development Plan: Part 1 of 2:
  - High-level design.
  - Development steps and timing.

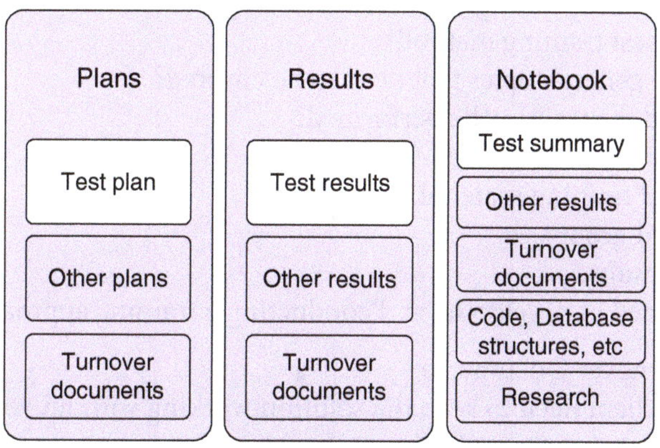

Figure 6–1 Relationships of Deliverables and Notebook

- Test start and stop.
- Training start and stop.
- Implementation start and stop.
- Team meetings.
- Customer meetings.
- Baseline schedule: GANTT chart or similar approach.

■ Development Plan: Part 2 of 2:
- Final schedule compared to baseline schedule.
- Lessons learned in developing a schedule.

Assignment 3. Test Plan

■ Test Plan: Part 1 of 2:
- What to test?
- Where is the test environment?
- When to test?
- Who will complete the test?
- Sample test scripts.
- Retest strategy.

■ Test Scripts and Test Results: Part 2 of 2:
- Create scripts.
- Perform testing.
- Document results.
- Lessons learned in developing and executing a testing strategy.

Assignment 4. Quantification Plan

■ Quantification Plan: Part 1 of 2:
- How did you originally measure the problem?
- How will you measure improvement?
- How will you gather data?
- When will you start gather the data and for how long?
- Live system or proof of concept.
- What assumptions?

■ Quantification Results: Part 2 of 2:
- Gather/analyze/summarize results.
- Lessons learned in measuring the impact of a solution.

Assignment 5. Training Plan

■ Training Plan: Part 1 of 2:
- Identify the audience.
- How many different user groups need training?
- What is the best training method?
- What are the general topics that need to be covered?
- When should the training be performed?

■ Training Documents and Results: Part 2 of 2:
- Create formal training material.
- Train targeted groups.
- Document results.
- Lessons learned in developing and conducting a training approach.

Assignment 6. Turnover Documents:

- What does the client need to keep the solution working without you?
- Hardware/software configuration?
- Design documents and source code.
- Maintenance agreements?

- Training manuals.
- Point of contact information.
- Formal customer acceptance.

Assignment 7. Comprehensive Team Notebook:

- Electronic copy of final presentation.
- Project and development schedule with completion dates.
- Supporting documents for testing, training, and quantification.
- Code, database structures, and so on.
- Other relevant data as determined by the team.

The assignments are listed as separately developed components and are typically assigned to team members individually. However, careful planning of the assignments can provide the opportunity to develop several of the assignments at the same time and in some cases use overlapping steps. For example, once an agreement is reached on the solution, team members should begin work on plans for testing, training, quantification, and possibly turnover documents. Refinements may be necessary as the solution and procedural changes are finalized and developed.

Similar parallel opportunities may exist for the results portion of the assignments. It may be possible to use test steps or training exercises to gather data for validating improvements that support the business case constructed in the first semester. Also turnover documents can start to be compiled as soon as the solution is identified.

These completed assignments become the basis for the final presentation at the conclusion of the semester. Chapter 7 provides a generic final presentation representing the results of the assignments.

The activities in Senior Design Project II assume that the project was implemented at the client's business during the semester. A completed implementation is the only unambiguous way to measure the impact of the solution on the business. However, implementation by the client does not always happen. A variety of issues may prevent this final step. Reasons include lack of time to implement, lack of funds if the solution requires a cash outlay, or client choice. In some cases the client will opt to implement the improvements at a later date, well after the team has ended their engagement with the client.

The team must still complete the activities for Senior Design Project II. In the situation where the solution is not implemented the team should complete the activities as a proof of concept. This approach includes completing all the assignments such as testing, training material, and turnover documents. The training and turnover documents become important when the client decides to implement the improvement after the team engagement has ended. These should have complete instructions on hardware and software requirements and detailed implementation steps.

There are numerous ways this proof of concept could be executed. The main issue is the lack of measurements related to impact of the solution. The team should rely on research and a test environment to replicate the process and estimate the impact of the solution. The extent of research must be sufficient to support the forecast of the improvement. The level of research is similar to the discussion of evidence in Chapter 2. It should be sufficient to convince the reviewers during the final presentation.

SCORECARD FOR SENIOR DESIGN PROJECT II

As a guide during the semester, the teams can use the same presentation scorecard that will be used by the judges for the final presentation. As in the first semester, the scorecard has two major components, presentation and content. The presentation portion, accounting for 15% of the score, is identical to that used in the first semester and is shown below.

Presentation is Clear	0	6	7	8	9	10
Effective use of visual media Media and presentation are consistent and clear						

Team is Convincing	0	6	7	8	9	10
Demonstrates enthusiasm and conviction Able to answer questions from judges						

The content portion of the scorecard is significantly different that that used in the first semester and reflects the elements necessary to support the presentation of a completed project. Many of the elements in the content section are elements one would find in most information technology projects.

Original Business Process	0	6	7	8	9	10
Enterprise business and process workflow is briefed Quantified business process presented Compelling business case for change is explained Implementation challenges presented						

IT Solution	0	12	14	16	18	20
IT solution is clearly described Solution is innovative and addresses major issue(s) All 4 concentrations adequately addressed						

Changed Business Process	0	12	14	16	18	20
Changes to the original business process are described Quantified impact of changed process explained						

Solution Implementable	0	12	14	16	18	20
Project is finished and acceptable to the sponsor Implementation challenges successfully addressed Documentation is complete (esp. testing and training) IT solution sustainment is addressed						

Demonstration	0	6	7	8	9	10
IT demonstration accomplishes stated objectives						

In the final presentation the team must show that they provided a positive impact for the client. Discussing the elements during the final presentation shown in Chapter 7 typically shows this evidence.

QUESTIONS AND CASE STUDY FOR CHAPTER 6

1. In comparing the scorecard for Senior Design Project I and Senior Design Project II, which elements are present in both and which elements are introduced for the second semester?
2. Most of the assignments listed in the chapter have two parts. Given the time constraints of the semester, which portions of the assignments might be conducted in parallel, that is, overlapping, rather than in a serial fashion?
3. In the situation where the client decides to implement the solution after the team completes the course, which elements of the turnover documents might need more detail than if the team was doing the implementation?

Case Study: At the conclusion of Senior Design Project I the team recommended a two-part solution. Each part could be implemented independently but either one implemented alone would reduce the impact of the business case for change to only a 45% improvement. The client is considering implementing only one part of the solution since the technology in both parts is new to her and the associated change in processes, although minor, is a concern. The client has been engaged and the relationship with the client is not an issue.
This is the first week of Senior Design Project II. What actions or plans could the team consider to improve the likelihood of the adoption of both parts of their solution?

CHAPTER

7 Sample Senior Design Project II Presentation

Chapter 7 shows a sample presentation given at the conclusion of Senior Design Project II. Similar to the presentation shown in Chapter 4, the presentation shows the basic elements that are typically included in a presentation.

CONSOLIDATING THE PROJECT INTO A COMPELLING PRESENTATION

The team should be building pieces of their final presentation as they progress through their project. There is rarely sufficient time to build the final presentation in just the last few weeks. By the end of the semester the team has presented many of the final presentation elements in various status reports to the class and faculty. These status reports provide an opportunity for other teams to contribute advice on both the technical solution and the material being presented. It is prudent for the team conducting the presentation to take notes for potential improvements in both the solution and the presentation.

Two methods are used to help teams improve their presentation material and get accustomed to public speaking. First, there are several relatively formal team presentations scheduled during the semester. These are opportunities for other teams to act as judges using the scorecard for the semester. This helps the presenters by giving them feedback based on the scorecard elements. It also helps the students understand what is on the scorecard.

A second approach is having each team self-evaluate the status of their project relative to completeness using a scorecard. Rather than using the scorecard as a point system, the teams use the scorecard as a gauge on the scale of "not started" thru "underway" to "completed and documented."

The draft and subsequent final presentations, including the script for each presentation element, will require careful consideration as to content. The typical presentation will be 15 minutes long, including introductions of the team members. Incorporating video and audio elements must be timed and rehearsed to coincide with the presentation. There is no opportunity for a retake in the final presentation.

In Chapter 4, of this workbook, we walked through a rather generic end-of-semester presentation from Senior Design Project I. What follows is a review of a completed project for Senior Design Project II. Similar to the presentation in Chapter 4, this presentation is generic and quite basic. Team presentations will be more detailed, contain more graphics, and deliver a compelling demonstration of the solution and its positive impact on the business process under analysis.

As in Chapter 4, this particular presentation is the same non-profit organization. The elements that must be addressed by the student team in course of the Senior Design Project II are similar to those that would be addressed in a for-profit business. For perspective, the business under review is a non-profit, charitable organization that provides short-term housing for families. Their housing portfolio is comprised of 150 single-family, townhouse, and condominium properties located in a suburban metropolitan area.

For brevity, several basic slides have been omitted. These include a presentation agenda, pictures of team members, and a concluding slide. In the formal presentation all team members are identified including a picture of each member and their role on the team.

SAMPLE TO-BE (FUTURE STATE) PRESENTATION

The sample presentation begins with introductory material similar to that presented in Senior Design Project I, such as team organization, context of the business, and the key issue. The business and team are introduced in Figure 7–1 through 7–3. In this case the key issue is "property maintenance and property availability" shown in Figure 7–4. Figures 7–5 through 7–16 discuss the solution, the implementation and the impact of the project on the operation.

The presentation starts with a graphic indicating the client business. The first four slides in this sample presentation are similar to the introduction prepared in the first semester. This approach might change if the theme of the process improvement is more important than the client business. This alternate approach can make a dramatic statement early in the presentation.

The recipients of the presentation, at this point of the presentation, have a clear perspective of business environment and the issue being addressed. Up to this point the presentation material may be similar to that used in the first semester, although significantly enhanced with details the team has gathered in the ensuing analysis.

This sample presentation is very basic and is not a model for a particular solution or project. Each team and project will allocate presentation time in a manner that will most appropriately convey its particular client solution.

● **Figure 7–1** Introduction—The importance of this slide is to build the initial view of the client by using an interesting graphic.

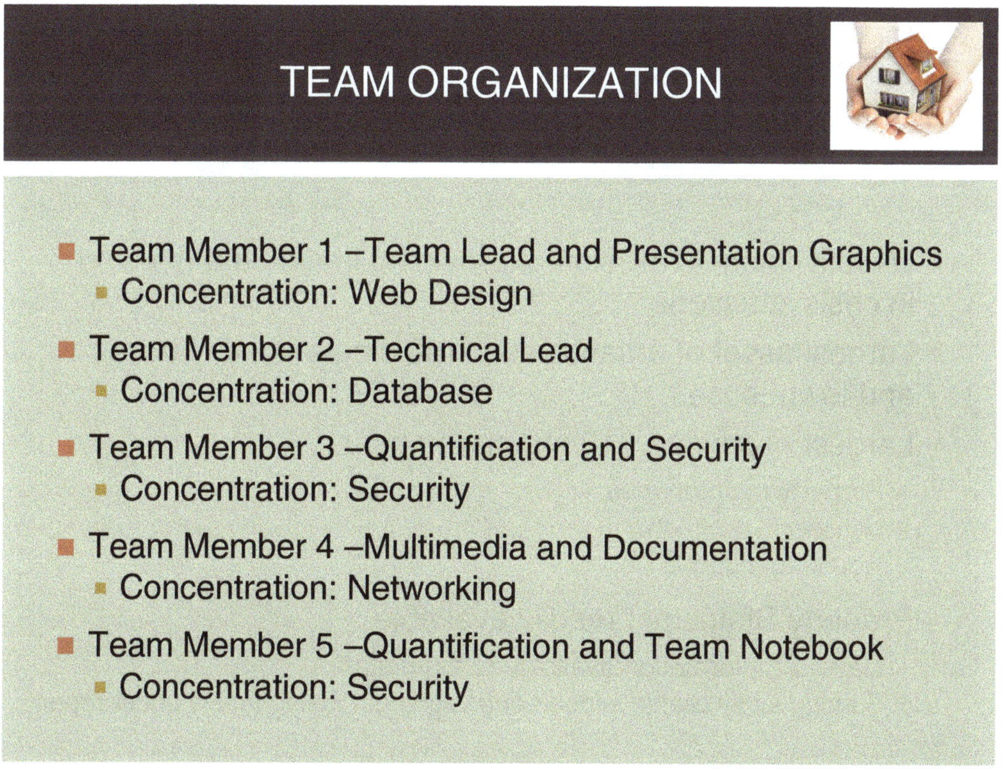

● **Figure 7–2** Team Organization—This slide introduces the members of the team and identifies the area each member will address.

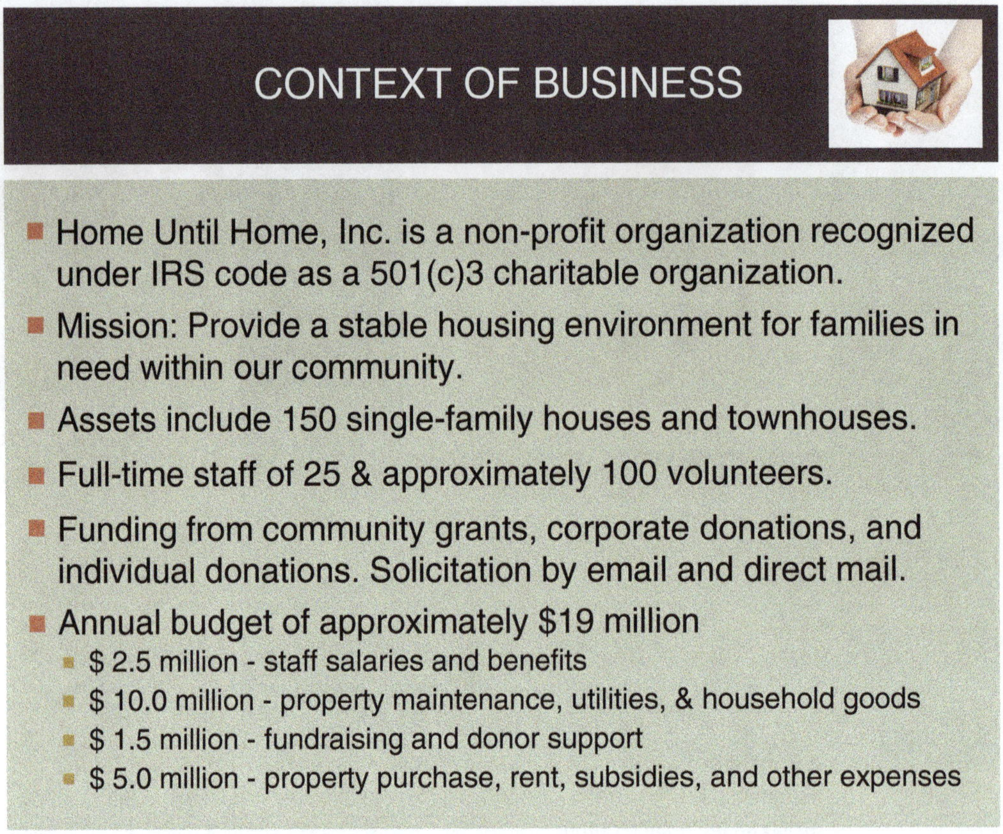

Figure 7–3 Context of the Business—The slide is a brief overview of the client. This is one of the few slides that may be repeated from the prior semester.

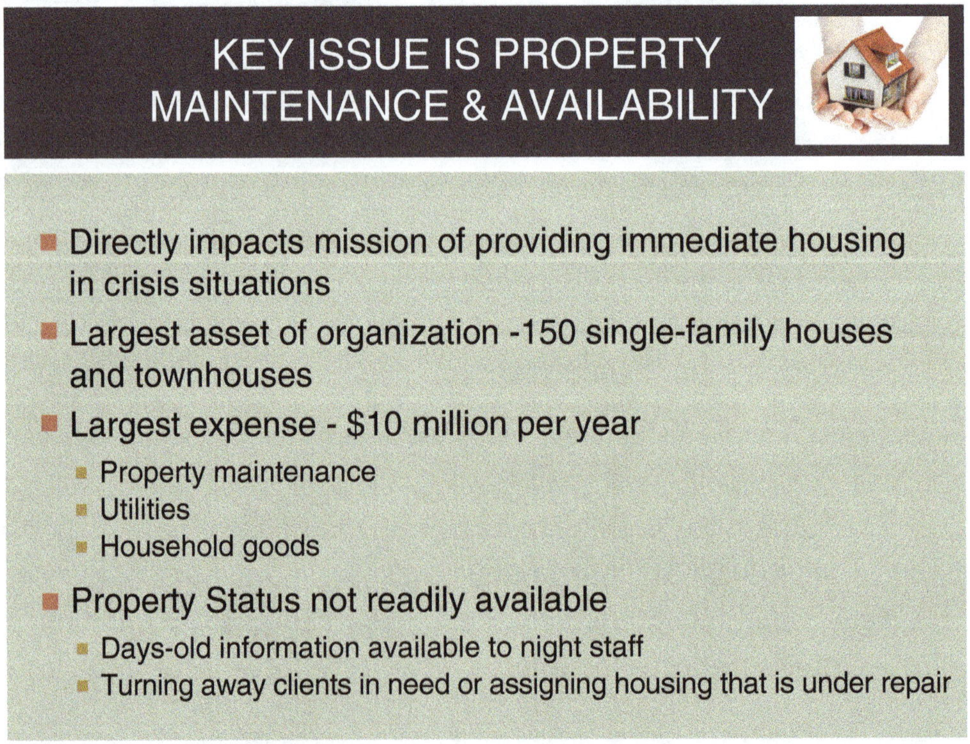

Figure 7–4 Key Issue is Property Maintenance and Availability—This slide presents the key theme of the project. The accompanying narrative by the speaker should be carefully scripted to convey how the team came to this conclusion. When the problem, identified in this slide, is understood, the solution to the problem is more readily understood.

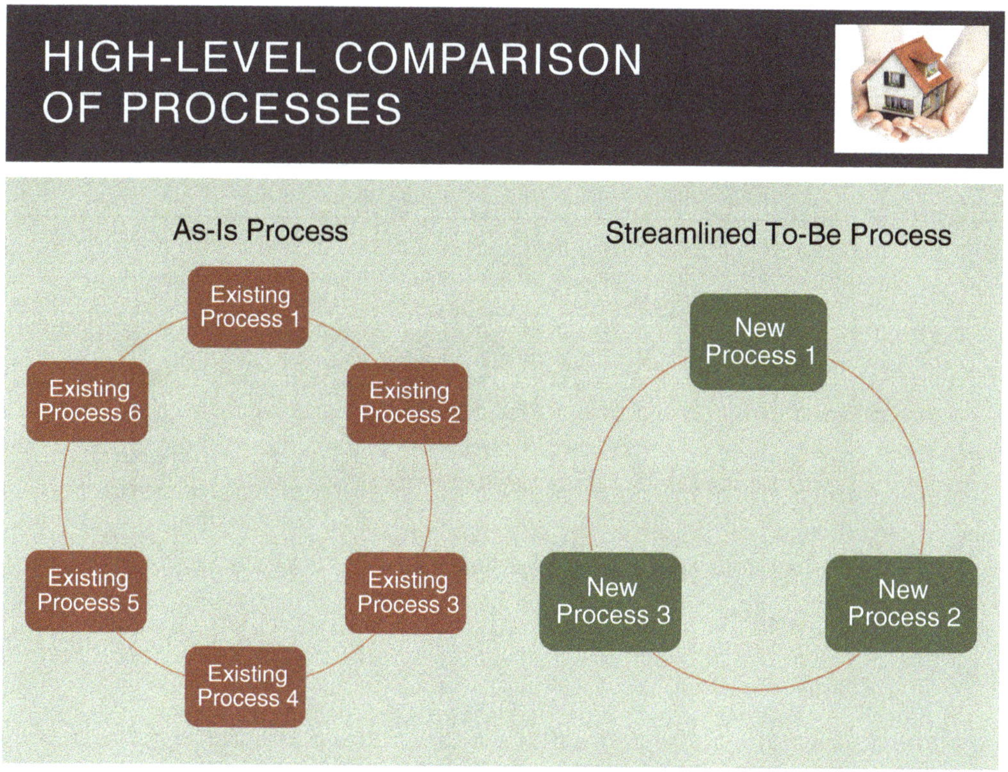

● **Figure 7–5** High-Level Comparison of Processes—A comparison of the existing and the proposed processes. There are a variety of approaches to describe the current and the new systems. This presentation would include a discussion of the changes, most likely at a high level to contrast the processes.

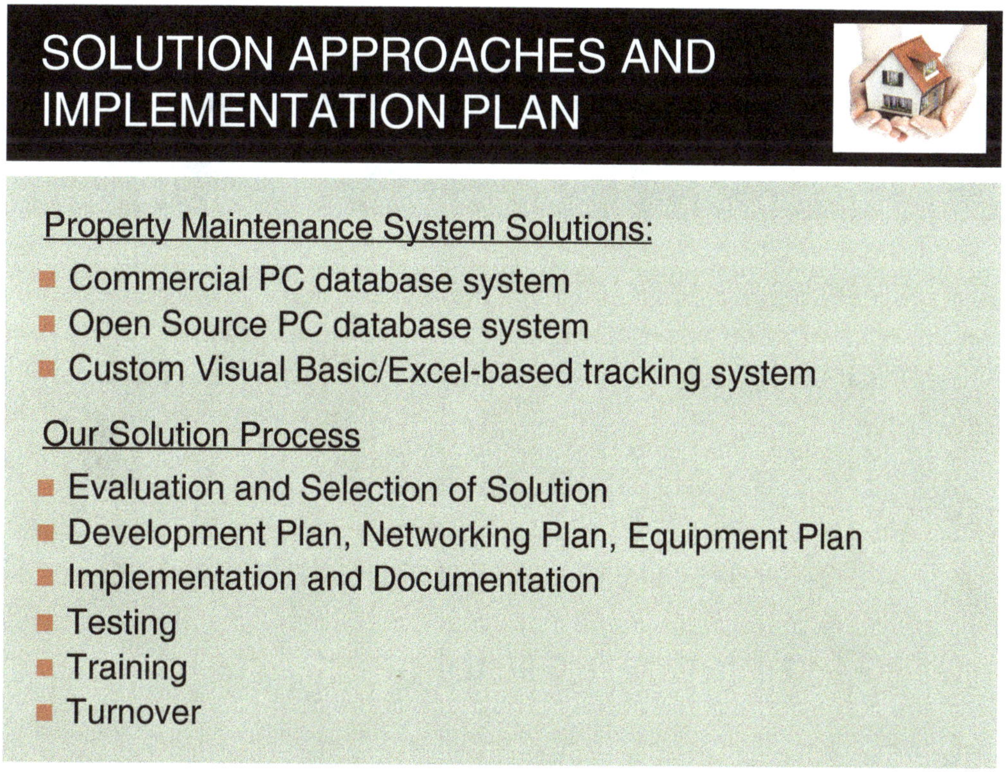

● **Figure 7–6** Solution Approaches and Implementation Plan—Based on the processes to be improved, the presentation shows the alternatives being evaluated and the steps the team took to select and implement the improvement.

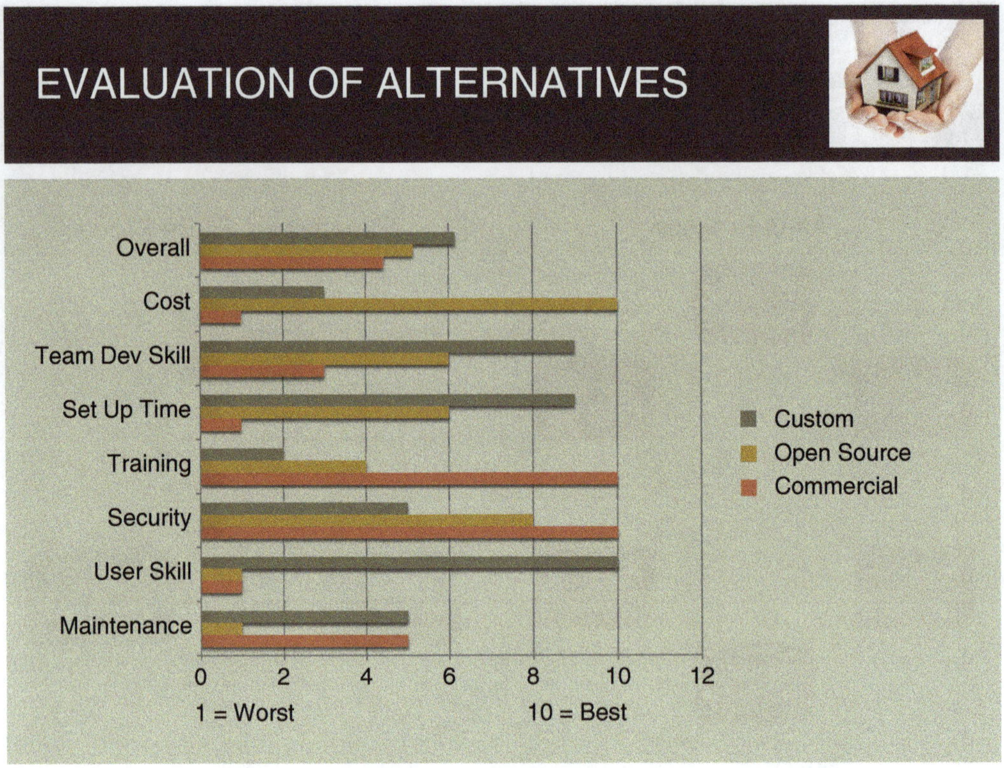

• **Figure 7–7** Evaluation of Alternatives—The presentation demonstrates that the team conducted an evaluation of the alternatives and arrived at a target solution based on a set of evaluation factors. The team would typically provide more details on the factors, the weighting, and the evaluation process. In this presentation the custom solution had the most positive score and was selected.

• **Figure 7–8** Development Plan—The development plan is introduced here so the reviewers understand the completeness of the solution and implementation process.

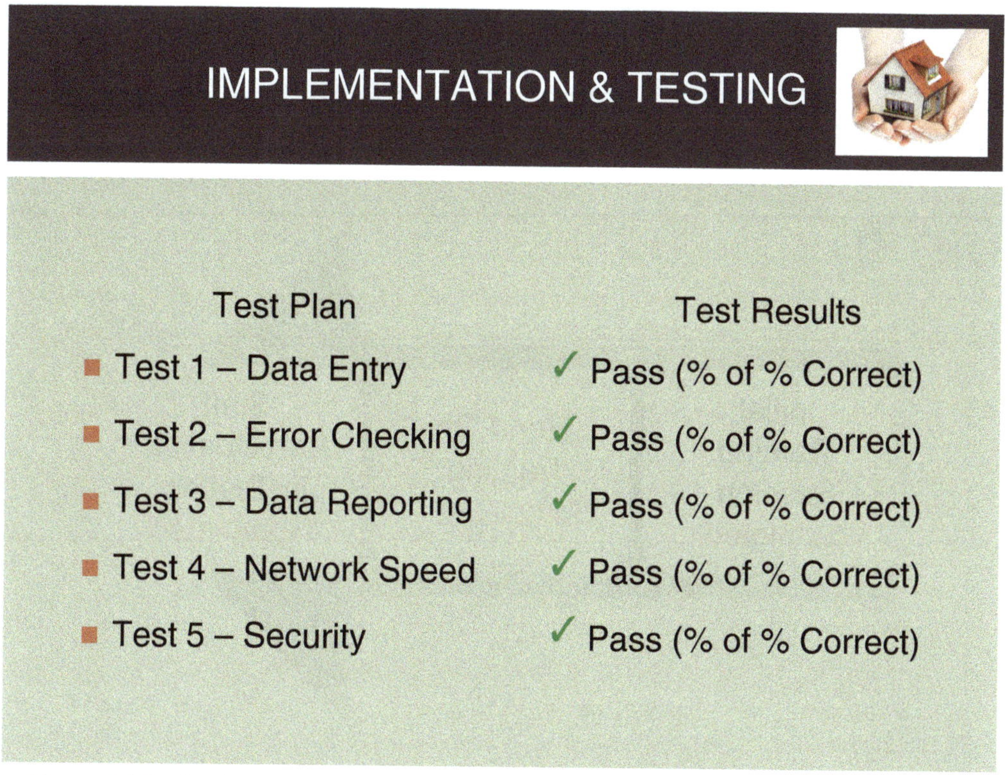

● **Figure 7–9** Implementation and Testing—Since this presentation is being made at the end of the semester, testing should be complete and results shown. This slide will be a summary of the detailed test procedures and data that will be documented in the team notebook.

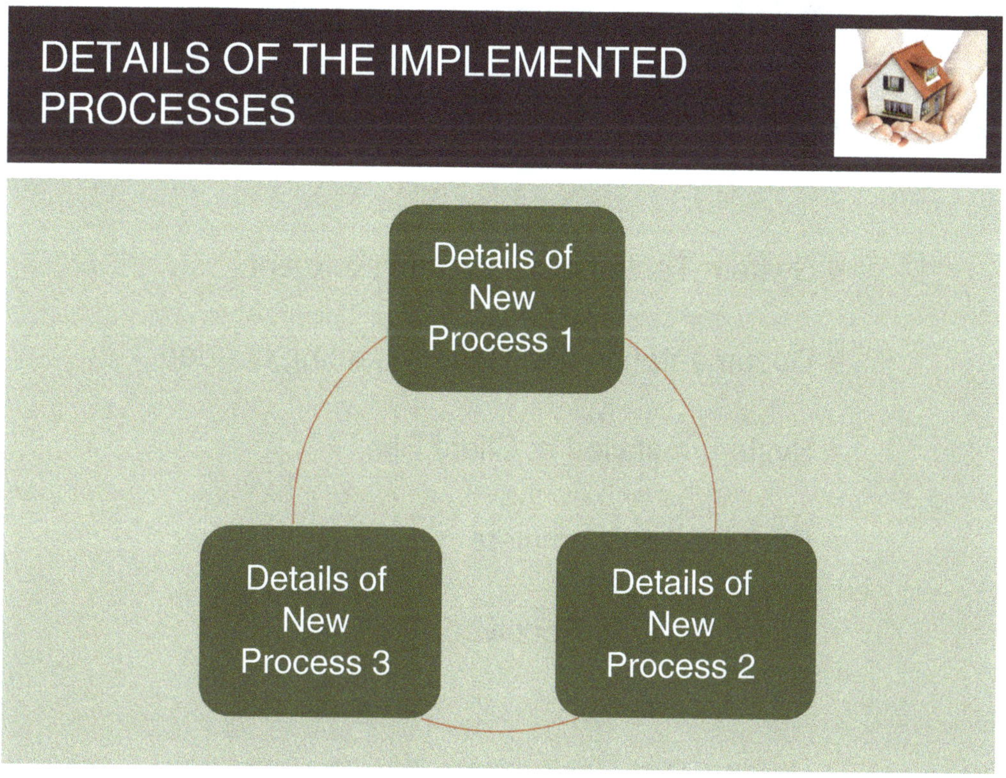

● **Figure 7–10** Details of the Implemented Processes—Although only one slide is indicated in this presentation, it may take several slides to show the improvements instituted and their effect on the process.

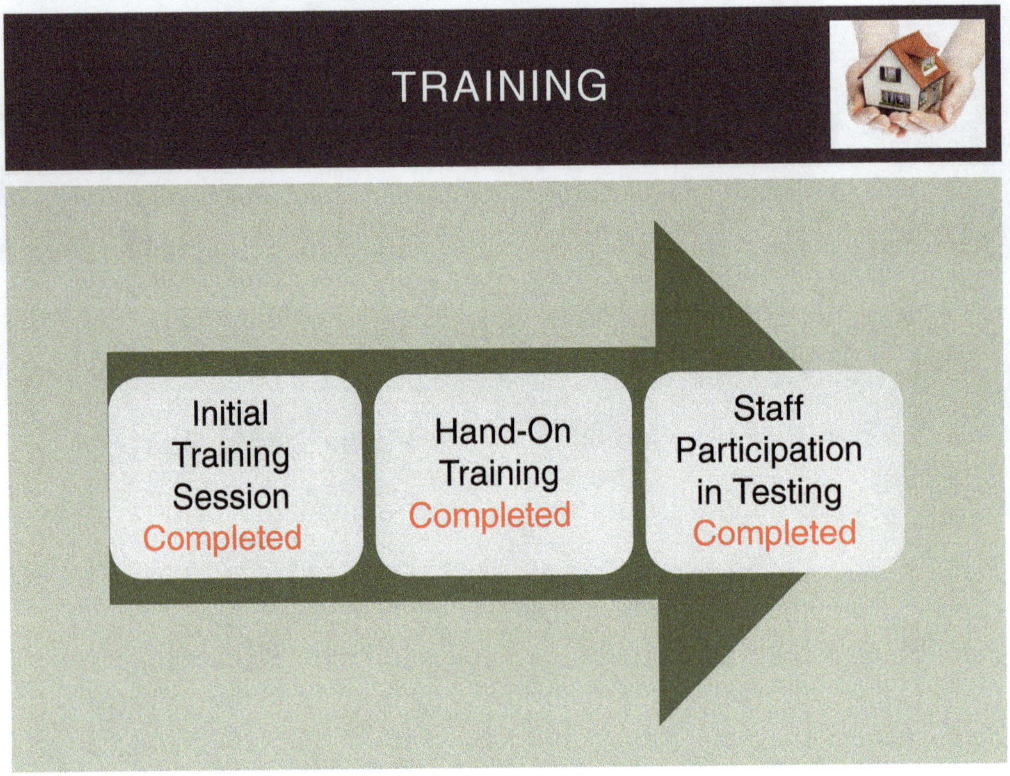

• **Figure 7–11** Training—This presentation includes a slide related to training, but many teams include a training video or show other robust training aids they developed to assist in the client's transition.

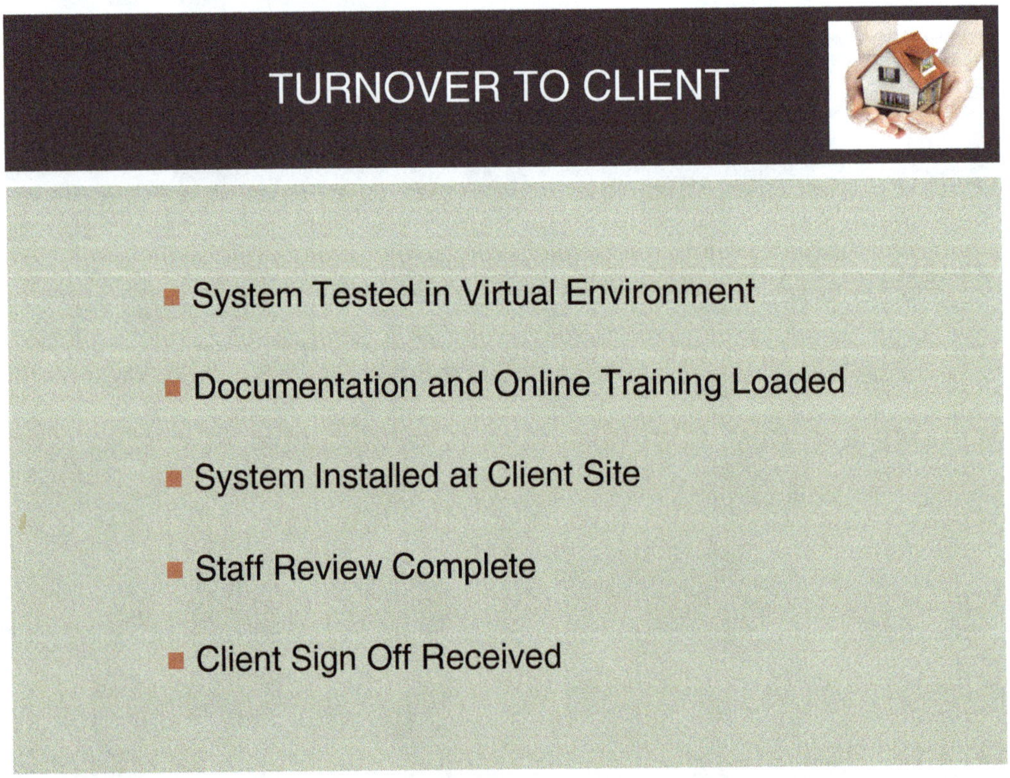

• **Figure 7–12** Turnover to Client—This Portion of the Presentation Related to Implementing the Improvements by Indicating the Client's Acceptance.

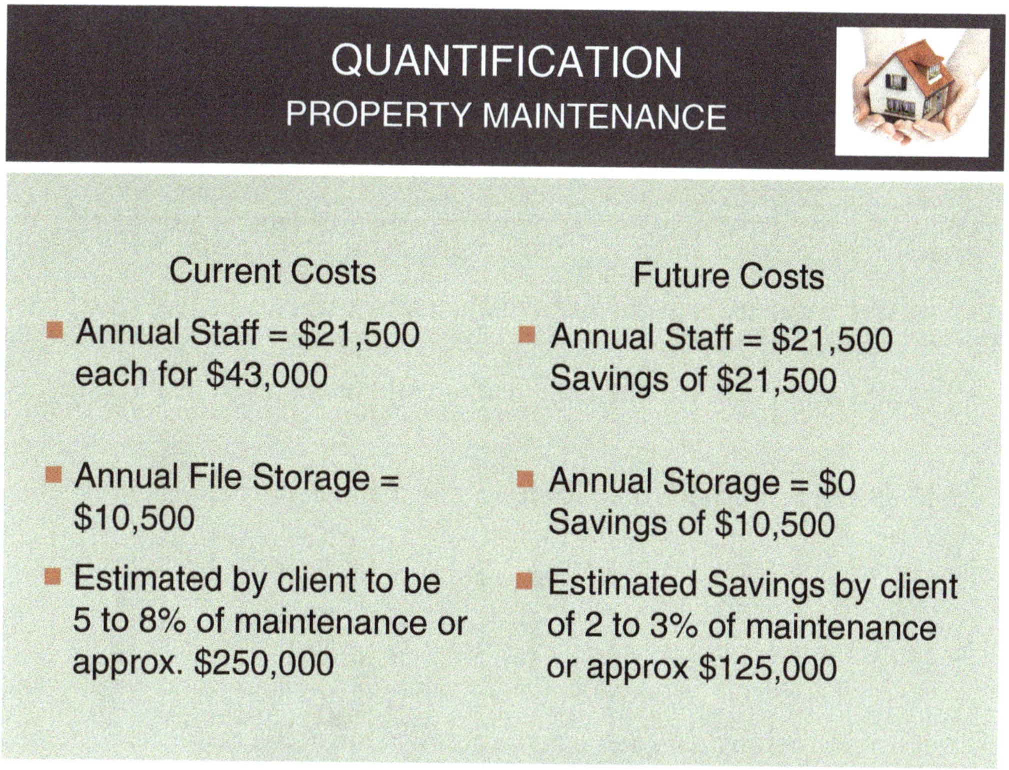

Figure 7–13 Quantification—The presentation moves from the implementation of the improvements to that of supporting the team's hypothesis that the improvement was beneficial for the client business. The comparison is between the initial quantification discussed in Chapters 2 and 3 compared to measurements of the new process.

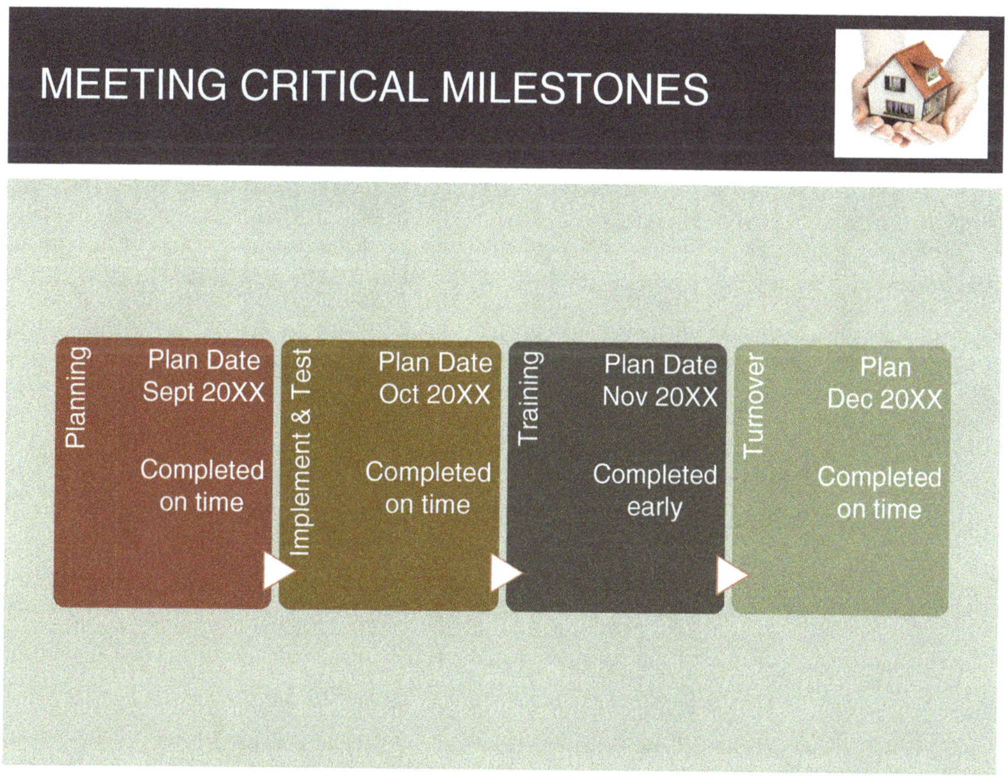

Figure 7–14 Meeting Critical Deadlines—In this presentation, the team was successful in staying on or ahead of schedule and has included that information in their presentation. This data would have also been included in the team notebook.

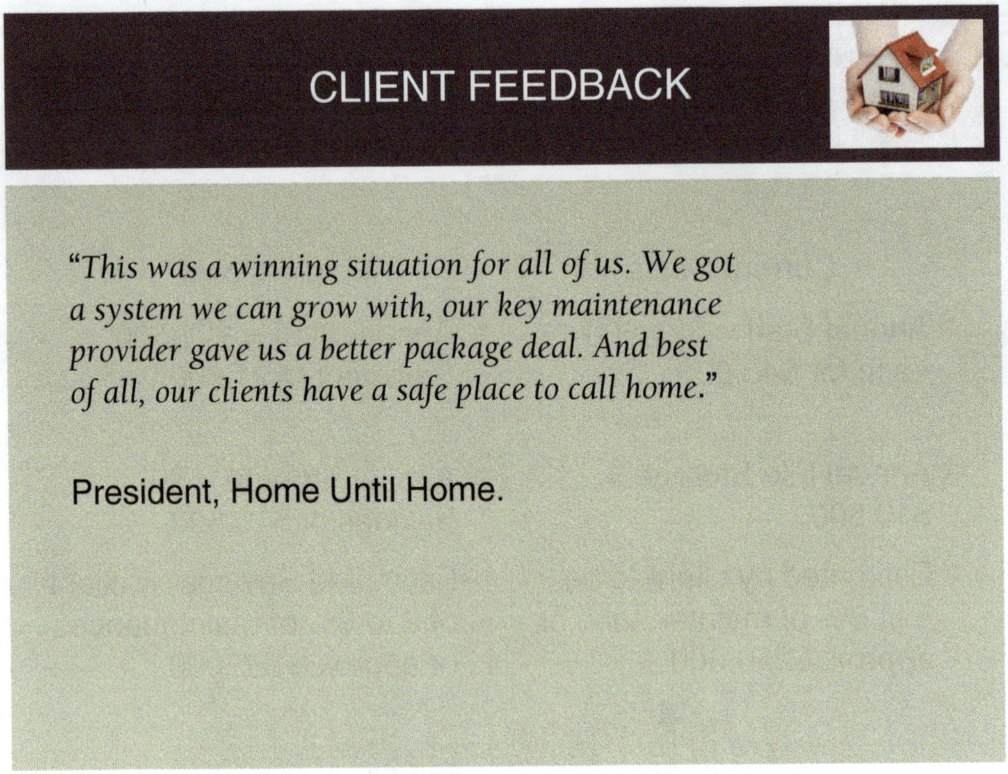

Figure 7–15 Client Feedback—This team concludes with a sterling quote from the client as support of the success of the project.

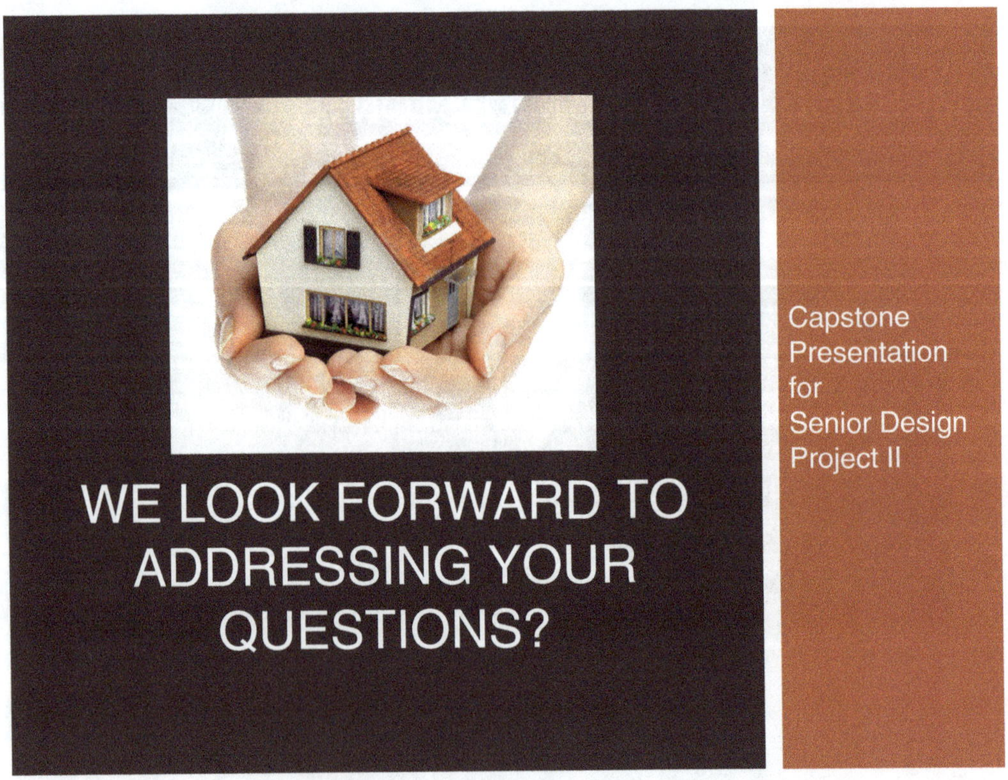

Figure 7–16 Conclusion of the sample presentation.

CLOSING OUT PART II

Senior Design Projects I and II provide a complete project from idea, through analysis, to implementation in a compressed time frame. These same steps can be a template for projects students will encounter in the work environment. These steps can be incorporated to ensure all the elements of the project are completed. The key ideas are

1. understanding the current business state,
2. measuring the costs of processes,
3. the forecasting of an improved future state, and
4. documenting a comprehensive solution for a client.

Index

T

W

SYSTEMATIC BOTANY MONOGRAPHS

VOLUME 59

Revision of Gasteranthus (Gesneriaceae)

Laurence E. Skog
Lars P. Kvist

THE AMERICAN SOCIETY OF PLANT TAXONOMISTS
17 July 2000

SYSTEMATIC BOTANY MONOGRAPHS

Vol. 1 [Taxonomy of Lygodesmia (Asteraceae), A. Spencer Tomb, 51 pp, 1980. ISBN 0-8357-0527-7] is out of print, but it can be obtained by placing an order directly with Out-of-Print Books on Demand, University Microfilms International, 300 North Zeeb Road, Ann Arbor, MI 48106-9976. Cite the catalog number: 2031944.

Vol. 2. The taxonomy of Cyperus (Cyperaceae) in Costa Rica and Panama, Gordon C. Tucker, 85 pp, 1983. ISBN 0-912861-02-9. US orders: $9.00; non-US orders: $10.00.

Vol. 3. The taxonomy of Saxifraga (Saxifragaceae) section Boraphila subsection Integrifoliae in western North America, Patrick E. Elvander; A revision of the genus Heuchera (Saxifragaceae) in eastern North America, Elizabeth Fortson Wells, 122 pp, 1984. ISBN 0-912861-03-7. US orders: $16.00; non-US orders: $17.00.

Vol. 4. The systematics of tuberous lomatiums (Umbelliferae), Mark A. Schlessman, 55 pp, 1984. ISBN 0-912861-04-5. US orders: $8.50; non-US orders: $9.50.

Vol. 5. Monograph of the Maurandyinae (Scrophulariaceae-Antirrhineae), Wayne J. Elisens, 97 pp, 1985. ISBN 0-912861-05-3. US orders: $12.00; non-US orders: $13.00.

Vol. 6. A monograph of the genus Lilaeopsis (Umbelliferae), James M. Affolter, 140 pp, 1985. ISBN 0-912861-06-1. US orders: $18.00; non-US orders: $19.00.

Vol. 7. Systematics of the Acutae group of Carex (Cyperaceae) in the Pacific Northwest, Lisa A. Standley, 106 pp, 1985. ISBN 0-912861-07-X. US orders: $13.00; non-US orders: $14.00.

Vol. 8. The systematics of Acmella (Asteraceae-Heliantheae), Robert K. Jansen, 115 pp, 1985. ISBN 0-912861-08-8. US orders: $13.50; non-US orders: $14.50.

Vol. 9. The genus Salix (Salicaceae) in the southeastern United States, George W. Argus, 170 pp, 1986. ISBN 0-912861-09-6. US orders: $20.00; non-US orders: $21.00. [Henry Allan Gleason Award, 1988]

Vol. 10. Systematics and evolution of Cordylanthus (Scrophulariaceae-Pedicularieae) (including the taxonomy of subgenus Cordylanthus), Tsan Iang Chuang and Lawrence R. Heckard, 105 pp, 1986. ISBN 0-912861-10-X. US orders: $13.00; non-US orders: $14.00.

Vol. 11. Systematics of the New World species of Marsilea (Marsileaceae), David M. Johnson, 87 pp, 1986. ISBN 0-912861-11-8. US orders: $10.00; non-US orders: $11.00.

Vol. 12. Systematics of Tetramerium (Acanthaceae), Thomas F. Daniel, 134 pp, 1986. ISBN 0-912861-12-6. US orders: $16.50; non-US orders: $17.50.

Vol. 13. Azpeitia (Bacillariophyceae): Related genera and promorphology, G. A. Fryxell, P. A. Sims, and T. P. Watkins, 74 pp, 1986. ISBN 0-912861-13-4. US orders: $9.00; non-US orders: $10.00.

Vol. 14. A monograph of Leochilus (Orchidaceae), Mark W. Chase, 97 pp, 1986. ISBN 0-912861-14-2. US orders: $12.00; non-US orders: $13.00.

Vol. 15. Taxonomy of Agastache section Brittonastrum (Lamiaceae-Nepeteae), Roger W. Sanders, 92 pp, 1987. ISBN 0-912861-15-0. US orders: $11.00; non-US orders: $12.00.

Vol. 16. A monograph of Nymphaea subgenus Hydrocallis (Nymphaeaceae), John H. Wiersema, 112 pp, 1987. ISBN 0-912861-16-9. US orders: $13.50; non-US orders: $14.50. [Jesse M. Greenman Award, 1988]

Vol. 17. Systematics of Frankenia (Frankeniaceae) in North and South America, M. A. Whalen, 93 pp, 1987. ISBN 0-912861-17-7. US orders: $11.00; non-US orders: $12.00.

Vol. 18. Monograph of the Eremolepidaceae, Job Kuijt, 60 pp, 1988. ISBN 0-912861-18-5. US orders: $8.00; non-US orders: $9.00.

Vol. 19. Revision of Tristerix (Loranthaceae), Job Kuijt, 61 pp, 1988. ISBN 0-912861-19-3. US orders: $8.00; non-US orders: $9.00.

Vol. 20. Revision of Cuphea section Heterodon (Lythraceae), Shirley A. Graham, 168 pp, 1988. ISBN 0-912861-20-7. US orders: $20.00; non-US orders: $21.00.

Vol. 21. Systematics of Coursetia (Leguminosae-Papilionoideae), Matt Lavin, 167 pp, 1988. ISBN 0-912861-21-5. US orders: $20.00; non-US orders: $21.00.

Vol. 22. Systematics of Antirrhinum (Scrophulariaceae) in the New World, David M. Thompson, 142 pp, 1988. ISBN 0-912861-22-3. US orders: $17.00; non-US orders: $18.00.

Vol. 23. Morphology and systematics of Paepalanthus subgenus Xeractis (Eriocaulaceae), Nancy Hensold, 150 pp, 1988. ISBN 0-912861-23-1. US orders: $18.00; non-US orders: $19.00.

Vol. 24. Systematics of Oenothera section Oenothera subsection Raimannia and subsection Nutantigemma (Onagraceae), Werner Dietrich and Warren L. Wagner, 91 pp, 1988. ISBN 0-912861-24-X. US orders: $10.50; non-US orders: $11.50.

Vol. 25. Malvaceae of Mexico, Paul A. Fryxell, 522 pp, 1988. ISBN 0-912861-25-8. US orders: $40.00; non-US orders: $42.00. [Henry Allan Gleason Award, 1989]